Focusing On...
Treasury of Mme. Alexander Dolls

by Jan Foulke

photographs by Howard Foulke

Published By **HOBBY HOUSE PRESS**
Riverdale, Maryland 20840

Table of Contents

	Preface	3
	The Beauty of Dolls	4
	Collecting Alexander Dolls	4-5
I.	Cloth Dolls	7-12
II.	Marionettes	13-16
III.	Composition Dolls	17-39
	Dionne Quintuplets	17-22
	The Small Composition Dolls	23
	Betty Face	24-25
	Princess Elizabeth Face	25-29
	Wendy Ann Face	30-33
	Margaret Face	33-35
	Individual Faces	35-39
IV.	Hard Plastic Dolls	40-84
	Maggie Face	40-43
	Little Women	44-45
	Margaret Face	45-48; 50-51
	Godey Lady Dolls of 1950	51; 54-55
	Glamour Girls of 1953	57-58
	Winnie Face	59-60
	Cissy Face	60-65
	Elise Face	66
	Individual Faces	67-68
	Alexander-Kins	69-74
	Lissy Face	74-78
	Cissette Face	79-84
V.	Vinyl Head Dolls	85-89
VI.	Scarlett O'Hara, a Historical Perspective	90-102
	Index	103-104

Front Cover: (Left) 15in. (38.1cm) Composition Kate Greenaway; (Right) 14in. (35.6cm) Hard Plastic Scarlett O'Hara. (*Both from Maxine Salaman Collection.*)

Frontispiece: (Left to right) Hard Plastic "Rosamund Bridesmaid" (*Edna Black Collection*); 18in. (45.7cm) Hard Plastic "Glamour Girl" (*Maxine Salaman Collection*); 21in. (53.3cm) Vinyl Portrait "Scarlett" (*Virginia Ann Heyerdahl Collection.*).

Back Cover: (Above) Group of Hard Plastic "Scarlett O'Hara" dolls (*Virginia Ann Heyerdahl Collection*); (Bottom) 17in. (43.2cm) Dionne Quintuplets. (*Maxine Salaman Collection.*)

Dedication

To Maxine Salaman, whose enthusiasm for the dolls created by Madame Alexander is infectious.

Acknowledgements

To my friends Edna Black, Charles Bolton, Barbara Crescenze, Marjorie Darrah and Marjorie Yocom, Rosemary Dent, Vivian Flagg, Virginia Ann Heyerdahl, Joanna Ott, Maxine Salaman, Rhoda Shoemaker, Virginia Slade and Virginia Yeatman: Many thanks for your willingness to share your dolls with others by allowing us to photograph them for this book. Only through generosity such as yours is a project like this possible. Catalog illustrations and quotes from Dionne Quintuplet booklet used with permission of the Alexander Doll Company.

© 1979 by Jan Foulke

All rights reserved. No part of this book may be reproduced or utilized in any form or by any means, electronic or mechanical, including photocopying, recording, or by any information storage and retrieval system, without permission in writing from the publisher. Inquiries should be addressed to Hobby House Press, 4701 Queensbury Road, Riverdale, Maryland 20840.

Printed in the United States of America

ISBN: 0-87588-147-5

This lovely 23in. (58.4cm) hard plastic "Nina Ballerina" illustrates the beauty of Madame Alexander dolls. Her blonde floss hair is elaborately styled with a crown of pink artificial flowers. Her dress is of pink satin and net with gold rickrack trim. She has her original dress and wrist tags. (H & J Foulke.)

Preface

Since my awakening to the magic of Alexander dolls, I have come to admire and appreciate the dolls produced by Madame Beatrice Alexander in over 50 years of creating beautiful and functional dolls for the little girls of America. Hundreds of new and old Alexanders, of cloth, composition, hard plastic and vinyl, have passed through my shop; hence was born the idea for the second volume in our *Focusing On* series to concentrate on Alexander dolls. Eager and dedicated collectors of Alexander dolls have been delighted to share dolls from their collections with us. And what a wealth awaited our choosing! One of the most difficult tasks I have ever had was in deciding what to include in this book. And even after I was finished, I discovered "Lollie, the 'Lov-le-tex' Rubber Doll" from the July 1941 *Playthings* and the "Three Little Pigs" in composition from the November 1933 *Playthings*, which I will have to save for another time!

The dolls shown in this book have been organized first by the material from which they were made: cloth, composition, hard plastic and vinyl. In a case where two different materials were used, the doll is classified according to the material used for the head. The subclassifications are according to the faces of the dolls. Except for a few individual cases, the same face was used over and over for different dolls. This is a standard procedure with most doll companies. Such a doll receives her true identity with her special wig, facial decoration and, of course, clothes. No attempt has been made to show every doll with a particular face, as Madame Alexander has created thousands of dolls.

Dolls are credited to the collection to which they belonged when the photograph was taken. Since the photographs span a period of several years, some dolls have changed hands, one or many times.

Clothing labels are given in an abbreviated form. In addition to the doll's name, the tag usually also includes "Madame Alexander. All Rights Reserved. New York."

All of the dolls are in original clothes except in several instances where it is noted that the doll is wearing an exact copy of an original outfit.

The Beauty of Dolls

Since 1967 the cover of the yearly Alexander Doll Company catalog has carried the words: "The Most Beautiful Dolls in the World Are by Madame Alexander". No other company, American or foreign, has yet come along to seriously challenge this claim. The words *Madame Alexander* and *beauty* are inseparable. Even as a child Madame Alexander loved beautiful things as she does today. It was always, and still is, her goal to bring beauty into a child's life through the dolls which she creates. Just by flipping through a few pages in this book or gazing at a shelf of Alexander dolls in a store, one can readily see that she has achieved and is still achieving her goal.

Madame's flair for creating beautiful costumes has played a significant part in her tremendous success, and has helped place her dolls at the top of the list of those desired by collectors of modern dolls. Her achievement has been acknowledged many times, and especially when she won the Fashion Academy Gold Medal for 1951, 1952, 1953 and 1954. Her costuming is known for the elaborate attention given to detail in the design and execution of her doll outfits.

"There is no finer doll made than a Madame Alexander Doll" was used as an advertising slogan in the 1950s, and again there is no company to refute this statement. Madame Alexander has always insisted that her dolls be made of the best materials, using the finest craftsmanship available to produce the highest quality product.

Madame Alexander has always believed that a child's doll should be an educational tool, that it should contribute to a child's understanding of life, of people and of other times and places. Inspired by masterpieces of art and literature, Madame Alexander has created dolls which will expand a child's horizon. It has been her intention that seeing dolls inspired by great painters, such as Gainsborough, Renoir and Degas will motivate children to want to see the paintings for themselves, or that owning the "Little Women" or other dolls from literature will encourage children to read the book from which the dolls were taken. Not only does Madame Alexander turn to paintings and literature; her goal is to stimulate interest in other arts as well: theatre (Mary Martin), films (*The Sound of Music*), dancing (many ballerinas) and music (Jenny Lind). The educational process does not always stop with the naming and costuming of a doll either. It often continues with information given in a wrist booklet which accompanies the doll.

Madame Alexander also believes that a doll should stimulate a child's imagination. A doll is an extension of the child's world of dreams, and through the make-believe world of dolls a child can be in her imagination anything she wants—a prima ballerina, a princess, a beautiful lady, a movie star!

Collecting Alexander Dolls

Marks On Dolls

Not all of the composition and hard plastic Alexander dolls are marked on the heads and/or bodies. A great number of them have no mark on the doll itself. Of course, this presents a problem of identification when a doll is found without original tagged clothes. About the best that one can do under these circumstances is to compare the doll with a marked one having the same face style. In comparing, one must also consider the type of eyes, wig, quality of composition and body style. Even then, judgments must be made carefully as many composition Ideal dolls look like the Alexander "Princess Elizabeth"; many composition Arranbee dolls look like Alexander's "Wendy Ann"; and many companies made dolls that look like the small Alexander "Dionne Quintuplets." One collector said that all things being correct, i.e., hair, face, clothes, clothing label and possibly wrist tag, she never looks to see whether or not an Alexander doll is marked.

Quite a few of the 13in. (33cm) Alexander composition dolls with the "Princess Elizabeth" face are marked with a ⊕ on the head and a size number 13 on the body.

Clothing Labels

Clothing labels are important for identification purposes, especially if the doll itself is not marked. Labels usually give the name of the doll as well as the maker, but sometimes the label will give "Madame Alexander" only, without the name of the doll. Labels are usually located on the outside back neck of the garment, but can sometimes be found on an inside seam also. Some labels do not have the "e" on "Madame." Of course, if a doll has been played with, it might have the wrong dress, a replaced dress or the label clipped out. Comparison with dolls pictured in books would help to determine if the hair style, face and dress do go together. Sometimes the same doll will have different types of labels in original outfits. Some of the 14-15in. (35.6-38.1cm) "Little Women" are labeled simply "Madame Alexander," while others are labeled with the name of the doll. Sometimes a doll has a completely wrong label! One collector purchased directly from a toy store an "Edith, the Lonely Doll" unmistakable in her pink and white checked dress with a *Marybel* tag!

Sizes

When measuring dolls for comparison to published sizes, allow at least an inch differential, in sizes over 10in. (25.4cm) especially. And for larger dolls, even more must sometimes be allowed. Few of the 23in. (58.4cm) hard plastic dolls actually measure that large. Measurements can vary according to the person who is measuring, the style of hair, the shoes, the position of the doll, the tightness of the stringing and the hopes of the measurer!

Dates Of Manufacture

Dating dolls during the years for which catalogs are available—1942-1943 and 1952 to the present—is fairly easy. However, there were some dolls made which do not appear in the catalogs. Some of these were exclusive models for F.A.O. Schwarz, Marshall Field or Wanamaker. A helpful source for dating dolls during years for which there are no catalogs is the *Playthings* magazine, a trade publication for the toy industry. Since 1936 the Alexander Doll Company has advertised on the back cover of this magazine. Also there are many notes about Alexander dolls in the news section and pictures of them in articles about doll retailing. Another source is the magazine *Toys and Novelties*, but Alexander did not advertise in there much after 1936. Fortunately for us, we are near the Library of Congress where these magazines are available, although it must be noted that in the late 1940s and 1950s, the Library often removed the back cover when binding issues, so the Alexander ad is sometimes missing!

Another helpful source for dating is the store catalog. Sears, Montgomery Ward, F.A.O. Schwarz and other stores featured Alexander dolls in their catalogs.

Another clue to dating is the material from which the dolls are made. The Alexander Company switched from composition to hard plastic in 1948. Some of the first hard plastics were painted and look alot like composition. The finish on some hard plastic dolls is quite tan; others are rosy.

The wrist tags also help with dating dolls in years before catalogs were available. The gold cardboard octagonal tag with blue printing usually has the name of the doll on one side and "Madame Alexander" on the other. It is from the late 1930s and early 1940s. The green metallic clover with "Madame Alexander" on one side and the name of the doll sometimes on the reverse dates from about 1945 until 1950. Ocassionally one finds a square metallic silver tag from the same period. The gold metallic Fashion Academy Award tag was first used in 1951, so if a doll has that tag and is not shown in the 1952-1954 catalogs, then it is probably a 1951 doll.

Even using the catalogs one can sometimes have a problem dating a continuing doll series when the costumes were changed each year, but the catalogs carried the same photo for several years. In some instances, the fabric prints changed several times during a production year.

Vinyl Alexander dolls often have a date on the backs of their heads. This can be very confusing if the collector fails to realize that this date is the year that the face was copyrighted, and dolls issued in 1979 could still have a 1965 date on them.

Never Always!

Beware of making absolute statements that certain dolls *always* have or *never* have! Allow for the fact that there are possibly some variations in production when checking dolls for originality. "Rebecca" *always* has black hair, but I have seen

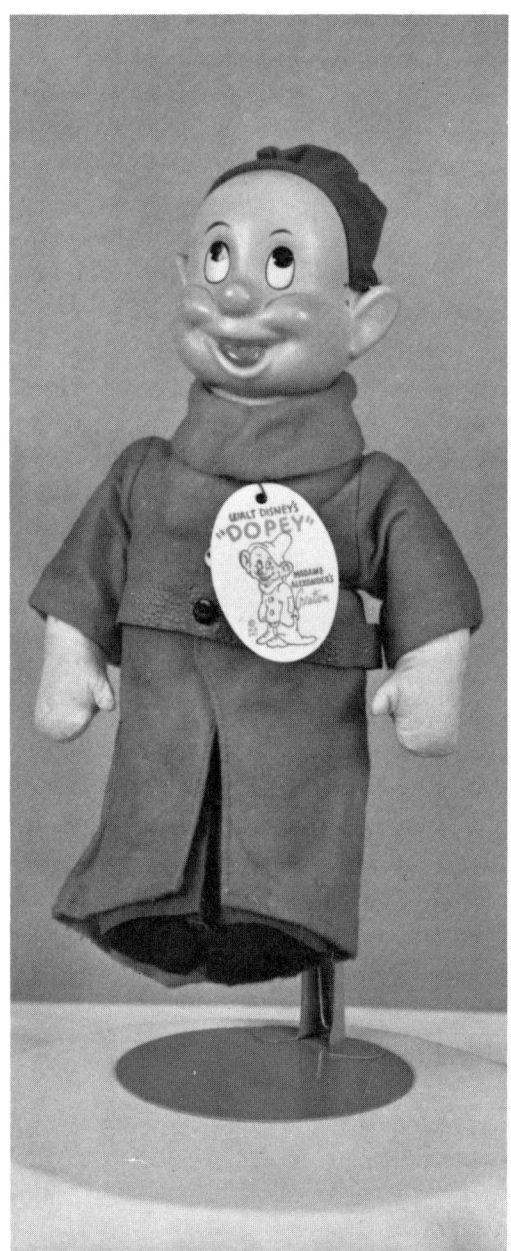

Walt Disney's "Dopey" by Madame Alexander. He is 13in. (33cm) tall wearing original felt outfit. His head is composition; his body is cloth. Advertised in the March 1938 *Playthings* as a tie-in with the movie *Snow White and the Seven Dwarfs*. (H & J Foulke.)

one new in the box with *auburn* hair! Alexander clothes *always* have square snaps, but a dress I looked at yesterday has buttons and buttonholes! There might be some variation in a doll's usual hair or eye color because the factory supply ran short, or in a clothing fabric which suppliers could not deliver in the quantity as promised. Perhaps there is a different shoe, low instead of high. These differences did occur and one must keep these possibilities in mind when examing a doll. It is not necessarily "wrong" because it is different. Some "McGuffey Ana" dolls came with straw hats; some came with none; some had organdy hats. And "Scarlett" does not always have green eyes.

I. Cloth Dolls

The first dolls designed and made by the Alexander sisters in 1923 when they started the Alexander Doll Company were soft. It was the intent of Madame Beatrice Alexander Behrman to manufacture dolls which would be lasting, not breakable like the German bisque-head dolls which had been brought to her father's doll hospital for repair. She also thought that the dolls should have attractive clothing which was both removable and launderable. One wonders what has happened to all of these early soft dolls; surely they were the beginning of the Alexander tradition and must have been available in a wide assortment of baby, child and flapper dolls. All of the four Alexander sisters participated in this first endeavor of the Alexander Doll Company, making bodies, painting faces and stitching the lovely little clothes, but it was Beatrice who was the spark of the company, who kept it going with her exclusive doll and clothing designs. And it was Beatrice who came to be known as Madame Alexander.

Perhaps many of these dolls from the 1920s have lost original clothes or had tags clipped out; perhaps also, some of them were not tagged. Since soft dolls have always been popular with children, it is probable that most of them were played with rather hard and were just disposed of instead of being saved for posterity.

The earliest identifiable Alexander cloth doll seems to be "Alice in Wonderland" from the classic book by Lewis Carroll. The trademark when found on her label is #304,488, which would date to August 1930; however, this number is not listed in Louella Hart's *United States Doll Trademarks*, though Hart does list #335,763 as "Alice in Wonderland" which was issued March 17, 1933, but I have never seen an "Alice" with this later number on it. This still becomes more confusing for dating dolls since Alexander announced in an August 1933 *Playthings* news feature that they had just recently been advised of trademark #304,488. This is three years later than the 1930 registry date. Perhaps they, too, were confused!

From the "Alices" extant it appears that the first ones had a flat cloth face with hand-painted features, large eyes and mouth in a surprised "O" shape. Some of these could possibly date before 1930 as an Alexander press release states that an "Alice" was made as early as 1923. However, a cloth "Alice" in *The Most Beautiful Dolls* by Jane Thomas, page 34, has a flat cotton flannel face with round eyes looking to the side and the #304,488 trademark on its tag.

In 1933, the film *Alice in Wonderland* was released and presented a marvelous tie-in for Alexander's "Alice" doll, and, of course, the company did not miss this opportunity for added publicity. The 1933 version of "Alice" had a plush or felt face just like the "Little Women" dolls, and

This doll appears to be the 1930-1933 "Alice in Wonderland" as she has a smooth cloth face, rather than a plush one. Her features are molded, but not so deeply as those on dolls from 1934 on. Her eyes are hand-painted and look straight ahead, although one does gaze slightly to the right! Her wig is of light yellow yarn in typical Alice style pulled back from the face and held by a blue hair band. Her blue and white cotton print dress has three rows of trim at the bottom of the skirt and her organdy apron has ruffles over the sleeves. Her shoes and socks are replacements. This "Alice" is 20in. (50.8 cm) tall, also supporting a pre-1933 date. Her dress is labeled:

ORIGINAL
ALICE IN WONDERLAND
TRADE MARK 304,488
MADAM ALEXANDER, N.Y. [sic]

(*Vivian C. Flagg Collection.*)

came in the 16in. (40.6cm) size. Gimbel's Department Store advertised them for $1.00 each. *Playthings* carried "Alice" features in both the August 1933 and January 1934 issues.

All of the cloth Alexander children from the mid-1930s had the same basic construction which was really very simple. They were 16in. (60.4cm) tall with a turning head having a mask face of suede cloth or sometimes of felt. Their lovely hand-painted blue or brown eyes, usually looking to the right, had an iris, pupil, several highlights, a red dot at the inner corner and painted upper and side lashes. Other facial features were one-stroke eyebrows and a bow-shaped mouth. The wigs were of mohair on a cloth cap, either glued or pinned to the head. Their unmarked bodies were of pink cotton. The torso was rectangular with the legs and arms sewn on. The thumb was separate on each hand. The faces were very similar, but seem to be reducible to two basic types: one usually used for "Alice" and "Little Women," the other for Dickens' characters.

The clothes were carefully made from washable fabrics. They were fastened with safety pins in the back. All contained Alexander labels which identified the character.

the film publicity would provide a great promotional opportunity for the stores carrying the Alexander "Little Women" dolls as they were an exclusive item made only by Alexander.

The "Little Women" dolls have cloth labels with the appropriate name. Some tags say "Trade Mark Pending" rather than "Copyright Pending."

LITTLE WOMEN
JO
COPYRIGHT PENDING
MADAME ALEXANDER, N. Y.

"Amy" has shiny blonde hair and pretty blue eyes. Her cotton print dress has pink and yellow flowers printed on it, a white organdy collar and pink ribbon streamers at the neck. (*Vivian C. Flagg Collection.*)

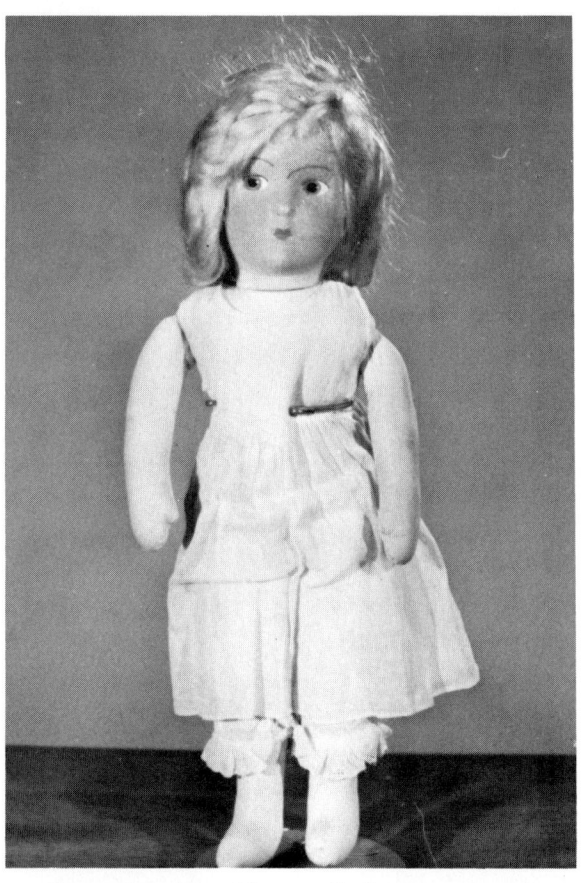

The undies of the girls were all of cotton or organdy constructed in one piece with long legs, having ruffles around the bottoms and a slip attached at the waist. From the photo one can study the neck joint, arm joint, shape of hands and feet, as well as the construction of the underwear. (*H & J Foulke.*)

The "Little Women" dolls appeared in 1933-34 with the trademark #344,080, November 24, 1933. They were advertised in the March 1934 *Playthings* as from the book by Louisa May Alcott and the RKO film which was released in 1933. Stars in this early version of the film were Frances Dee as Meg, Katharine Hepburn as Jo, Jean Parker as Beth, Joan Bennett as Amy and Spring Byington as Marmee. This was a group of four dolls of the daughters, but did not include a Marmee. Again,

In a photo feature in the March 1937 *Playthings* on page 104 and in a news feature on page 132, Madame Alexander announced "an entirely new version of these famous story-book girls of yesterday, done with a new type of head dress and new style clothing throughout." The dolls have yarn wigs which were apparently the new type of headdress referred to. Dresses appear to be cotton with puff sleeves and full skirts. Fabric prints are different from the earlier models. Two of the dolls are wearing aprons. I have never seen one of these versions "in person."

The book *Little Women* has remained a childhood classic for over 100 years, and since 1933 the "Little Women" dolls have been in almost continuous production by Madame Alexander. There have not been too many years when the "Little

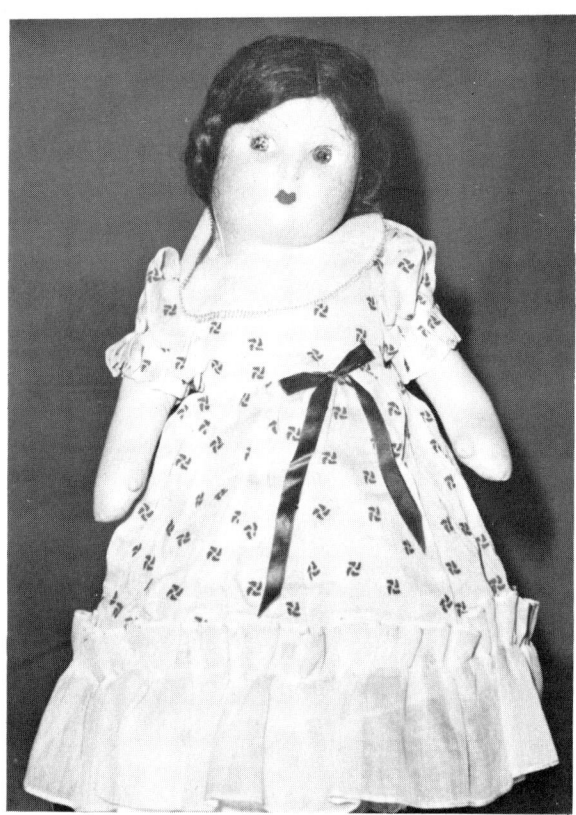

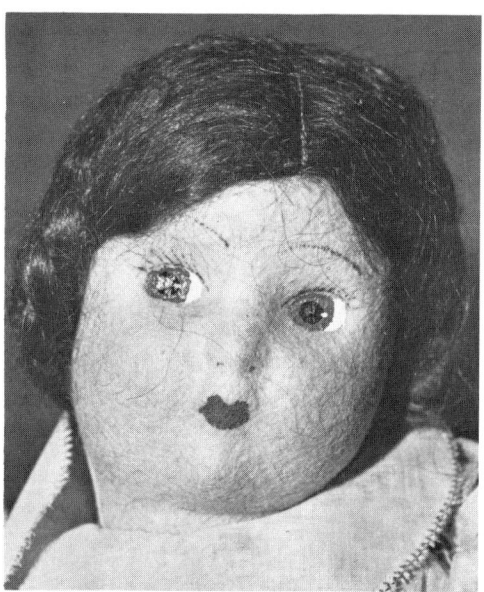

"Meg" is quite a surprise in that her face is of felt instead of the usual suede-type fabric. Her brown mohair is braided and brought to the top. Her dress is white organdy with a blue design. A white organdy collar and wide flounce on the skirt provide contrast. The close-up photo provides detail of facial painting as well as hair style. (*Virginia Yeatman Collection.*)

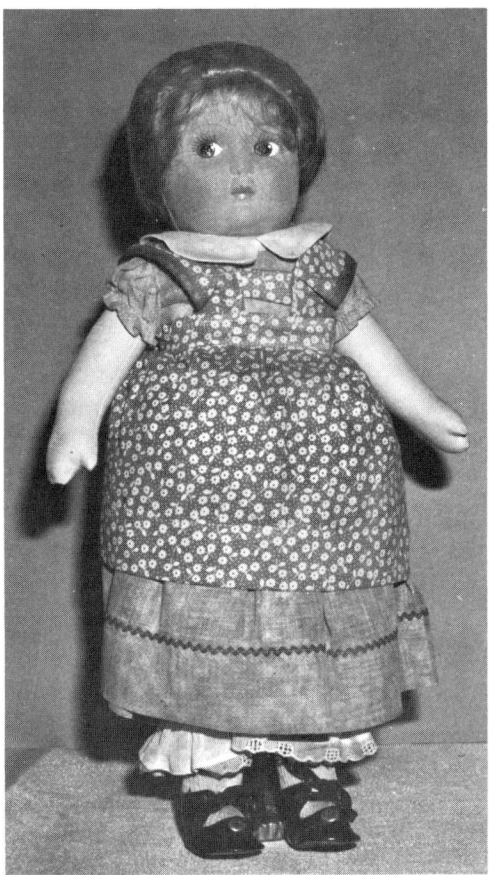

"Jo" has dark blonde hair pulled back with a red ribbon and bangs. She is wearing a blue and white organdy dress with a white collar and red rickrack trim. Her apron is a printed cotton with red background and white flowers. (*Vivian C. Flagg Collection.*)

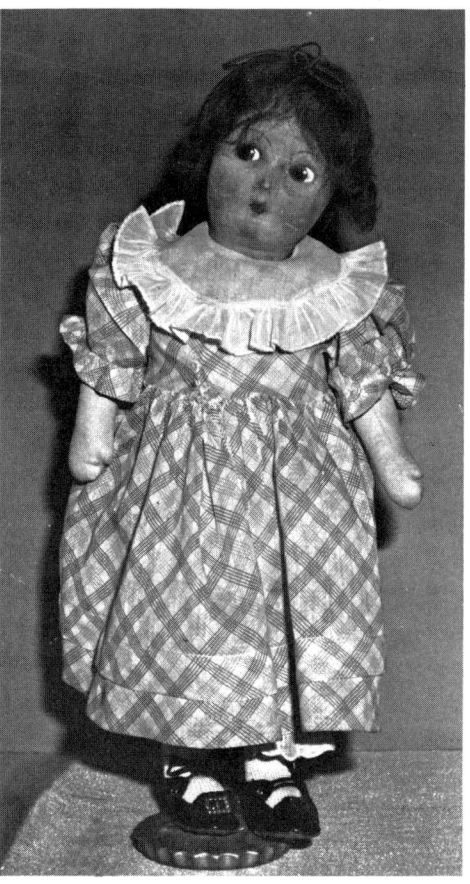

"Beth" has light brown hair. She is wearing a red and white organdy dress with a ruffled bertha collar. (*Vivian C. Flagg Collection.*)

Women" dolls were not part of the Alexander line. They were made not only in cloth, but also in composition and hard plastic in several different series. Currently they are being made in plastic with vinyl faces in the 12in. (30.5cm) size. The current 8in. (20.3cm) size is all of hard plastic.

The dolls, based on the characters from the classic novels of the English Victorian writer Charles Dickens, were announced by a news release in the June 1934 *Playthings*. At that time "David Copperfield," "Oliver Twist," "Little Em'ly," "Little Nell," "Little Dorrit" and "Tiny Tim" were announced. "Pip" from *Great Expectations* and "Agnes" from *David Copperfield* are not mentioned, but are known to have been made also. These characters would have been good tie-ins with the popular trend of the period towards movies based on the classics.

"Little Em'ly" is wearing a blue print dress with white organdy ruffles at the sleeves and pockets. Her bonnet is of matching fabric with an organdy ruffled brim. She has blonde hair and blue eyes. (*Marjorie Yocom Collection.*)

"Oliver Twist" is dressed in pants of a peach color with an attached white shirt. He wears a jacket of pale green with two small buttons and lapels which turn back. His brown cap sits atop a blonde mohair wig. (*H & J Foulke.*)

"David Copperfield" is dressed in an outfit of black and white plaid pants with an attached black and white checked shirt with a white collar. His jacket is black felt, as is his top hat. (*Marjorie Yocom Collection.*)

"Red Riding Hood" is certainly a rare find. She has a blonde mohair wig. Her dress is a red and white cotton print. Of course, her hooded cape is red! (*H & J Foulke.*)

This sweet girl is probably "Little Nell," although she has lost her tag. Most of the Dickens' girls have the same faces and similarly styled dresses with matching hats. The dresses are cotton prints of various designs with high waists, puffed sleeves and organdy ruffles on the bodice. This "Little Nell" is wearing a replaced straw hat and hose. (*Vivian C. Flagg Collection.*)

In addition to the "Alice," "Little Women" and Dickens' characters, other fictional and storybook dolls were made, but a complete list of these may be many years in the making. Two of these are "Babbie" from *The Little Minister* by James Barrie and "Red Riding Hood." I understand that there was also a series based on the poems of Henry Wadsworth Longfellow, but I have never seen any of these in photos or in person.

Some baby dolls in cloth were also a part of the 1930s line. The "Dionne Quintuplets" were made in cloth, but these are indeed rare. More easily found are the "So-Lite" dolls announced in a March 1937 release in *Playthings* as a "new development in the soft cuddly doll field." They are also shown in the 1942-1943 catalog. This large "So-Lite" doll is 25in. (63.5cm) tall with a mask face having molded features. Her large blue eyes look to the side; her tiny mouth is pursed. The wig is of curly strawberry blonde floss. She is wearing a pink chiffon dress with lace and rosebud trim. Her dress is labeled simply "Madam Alexander." [sic] (*Marjorie Yocom Collection.*)

The "Little Shavers" have mask faces with eyes painted to the side. Both dolls have fuchsia taffeta bodices and chartreuse organdy skirts with flounces at the hem. The sleeves have an organdy inset. Their wigs are of wool yarn: the larger auburn, the smaller blonde. The hats are flower bouquets with veils. The small doll carries her fuchsia taffeta reticule. The dolls are 15in. (38.1cm) and 11in. (27.9cm) tall. (*Vivian C. Flagg Collection.*)

Although not shown in the 1942-1943 Alexander catalog, a news release in the November 1942 *Playthings* refers to the "Little Shavers" as Madame Alexander's latest offering and hails them as a big success. The dolls were based on the paintings of Elsie Shaver's Victorian children which were seen by Madame Alexander at an art exhibition. They were also featured in the Alexander ad in the November 1942 and the January and April 1943 *Playthings*.

"Clarabell" dates from 1951 and is based on the generally lovable but sometimes cantankerous clown from the *Howdy Doody* television show. He is 19in. (48.3 cm) tall and made of white cotton cloth except for his black feet. He wears a gold and tan satin clown suit with a white ruffle around the neck. His hair is of orange yarn; his ears are of white felt; the eyes are flowers; mouth and eyebrows are red felt. His answer box which contained his horn is marked:
CLARABELL
BY
MADAM ALEXANDER [sic]
(*Vivian C. Flagg Collection.*)
This doll has also been reported in 29in. (73.7cm) and 40in. (101.6cm) sizes.

12

II. Marionettes

The March 1934 *Toys and Novelties* carried an advertisement by the Alexander Doll Company for the Tony Sarg Marionette Theatre. Tony Sarg was famous for his marionettes and for his puppet shows throughout the United States in the 1930s. One Alexander ad declared: "The whole world immediately thinks of Tony Sarg when it thinks of marionettes." Children were fascinated by his stories and marionettes, and since children enjoy acting out stories, they wanted puppets of their own to manipulate. Tony Sarg was a natural to help children because of his great interest in them and in his craft.

A news release in *Toys and Novelties* of April 1934 mentioned that Tony Sarg received hundreds of letters daily from children relating to marionettes and marionette shows. Questions in these letters led him to create a marionette theatre large enough to conceal operators. It even had a curtain and lights. With the theatre came puppets designed by Mr. Sarg, as well as plays and directions written by him. Additional puppets were also available. This entertaining as well as educational endeavor was "Manufactured and controlled exclusively by the Alexander Doll Company."

The construction of the marionettes was quite unique. All were about 11in. (27.9cm) or 12in. (30.5cm) tall. The heads were of composition molded with very well-executed character faces. The marionettes were advertised as simple to manipulate and tangle-proof. The wooden crossbar had a metal rod which hooked on to the top of the

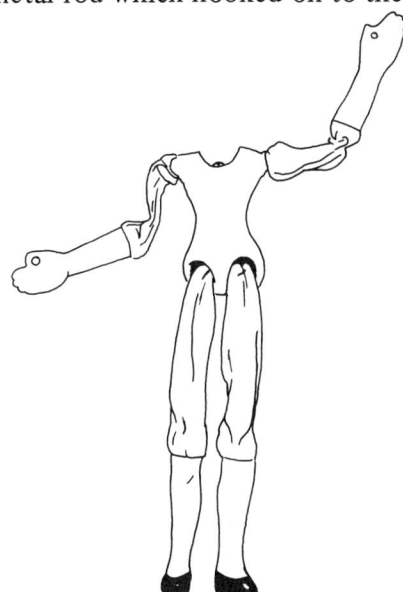

head and strings which manipulated the arms, legs and torso. The head was hooked onto the composition torso; upper arms and legs were pieces of cloth—slack, not stuffed; lower arms and legs were composition with painted shoes. The torsos were marked on the back:
TONY SARG
ALEXANDER
Heads were marked: TONY SARG

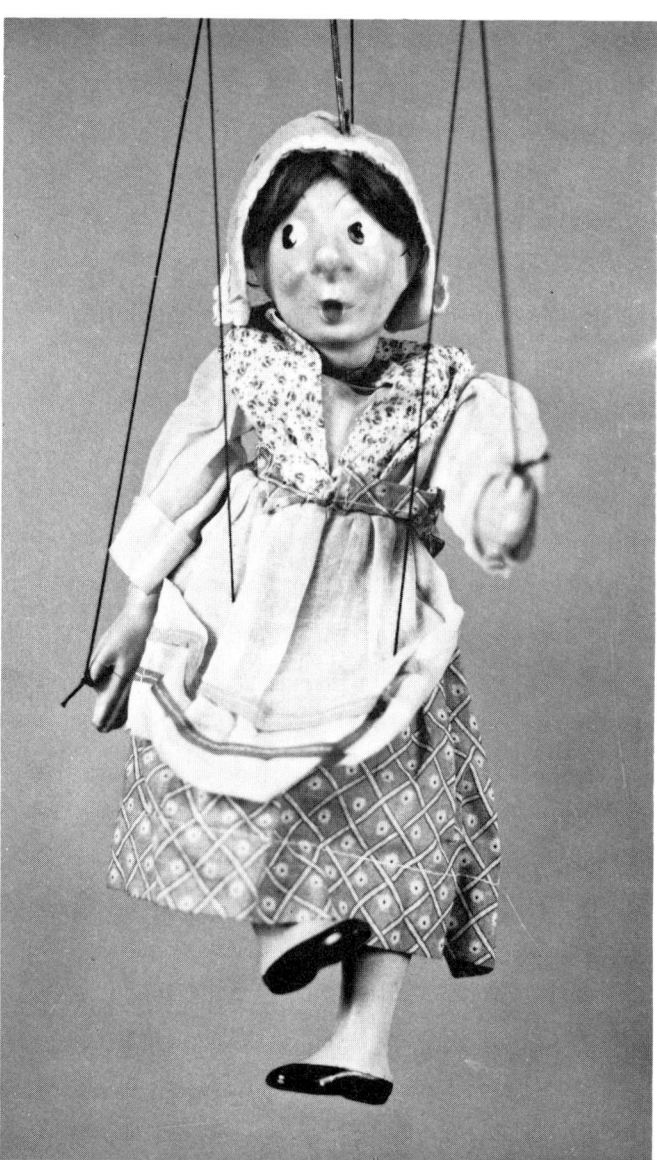

This marvelous character face has large round eyes looking to the side, a large nose, an "O" shaped mouth and high cheekbones. The mohair wig is brown. She is wearing a green print skirt, a flower print scarf and a white blouse, apron and Dutch cap. She is tagged only "Madame Alexander" so her identity is not known. (*Virginia M. Slade Collection.*)

Clothes tags when present usually said only "Madame Alexander." Sometimes the name of the character was given also.

These marionettes must have been a popular and profitable line for quite a few years as the June 1937 ad in *Playthings* listed a large selection of 11 plays and 32 characters:

Plays	Characters
Hansel & Gretel	Hansel, Gretel, Witch
Rip Van Winkle	Rip, Dame, Judith
Alice In Wonderland	Alice, Humpty, Tweedle Dum, Tweedle Dee
Tingling Circus 1	Clown, Dog
Tingling Circus 2	Riding Master, Ballet Dancer, Horse
Dixieland Minstrels	Sambo, Bones, Interlocutor
The Enchanted Prince	Prince, Princess, Gnome
The Three Wishes	Martin, Margaret, Fairy
Lucy Lavender's Hero	Lucy, Lawrence, Butler (Tippytoes)
Clever Gretchen	Gretchen, Mr. Archibald
Red Riding Hood	Red Riding Hood, Grandmother, Wolf

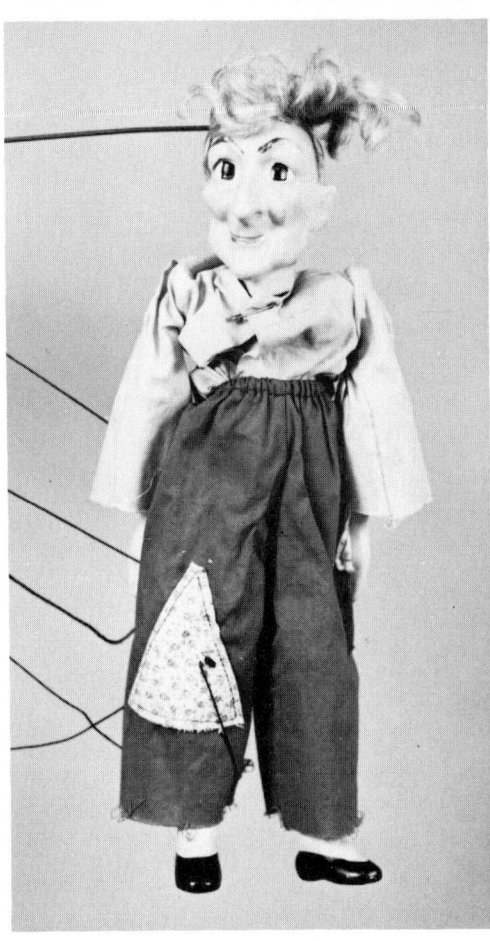

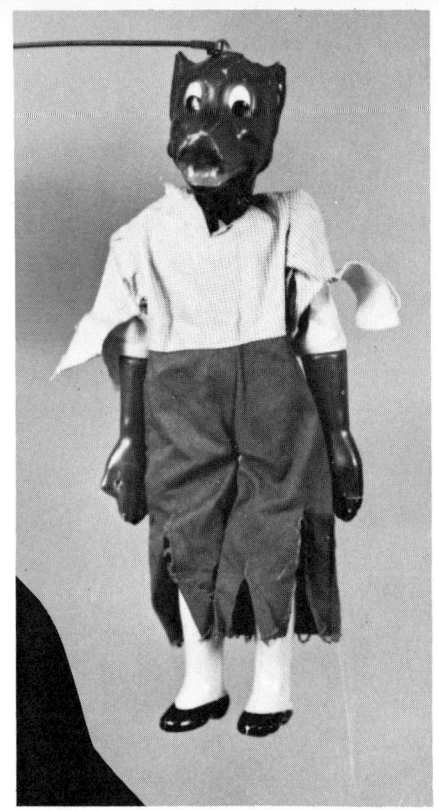

"Wolf" character from the Red Riding Hood play. (*Virginia M. Slade Collection.*)

Another interesting character face has a large nose, wide smiling mouth, angular face and thick eyebrows. His wig is of gray mohair. He is wearing brown patched pants and a gold shirt. His identity again is not known. (*Virginia M. Slade Collection.*)

"Hansel" has a round face, chubby cheeks and round eyes. His suit is one piece, and the remains of his hair is blonde. His clothing carries his name. (*Virginia M. Slade Collection.*)

This is "Tippytoes (Butler)" from "Lucy Lavender's Hero" play. The character face has molded hair, round eyes and a wide smiling mouth. The Butler's uniform has black and white striped trousers, a black dickey, a white shirt, a black tie and a black coat. (*The Doll Royalle.*)

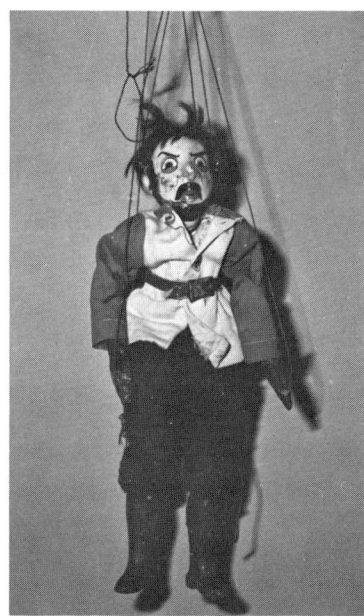

This character appears to be a pirate with a mean look. He has a painted beard, a large mustache and a black mohair wig. His eyes are large and staring; the eyebrows are heavy. He wears a green and white jacket with a brown belt, black felt pants and black painted boots. He is untagged. (*The Doll Royalle.*)

This girl has the same face as the "Prince." She is wearing a dress with a pink rayon skirt and sleeves and a blue velvet bodice with flower trim. Her wig is blonde mohair. She is untagged. (*The Doll Royalle.*)

"Prince" is dressed in yellow pants with an attached ruffled shirt, a blue coat and a medallion at his neck. His wig is brown mohair. He has his cloth label also:
           TONY SARG'S MARIONETTES
                    "Prince"
          MADAM ALEXANDER, N.Y. [sic]
(*The Doll Royalle.*)

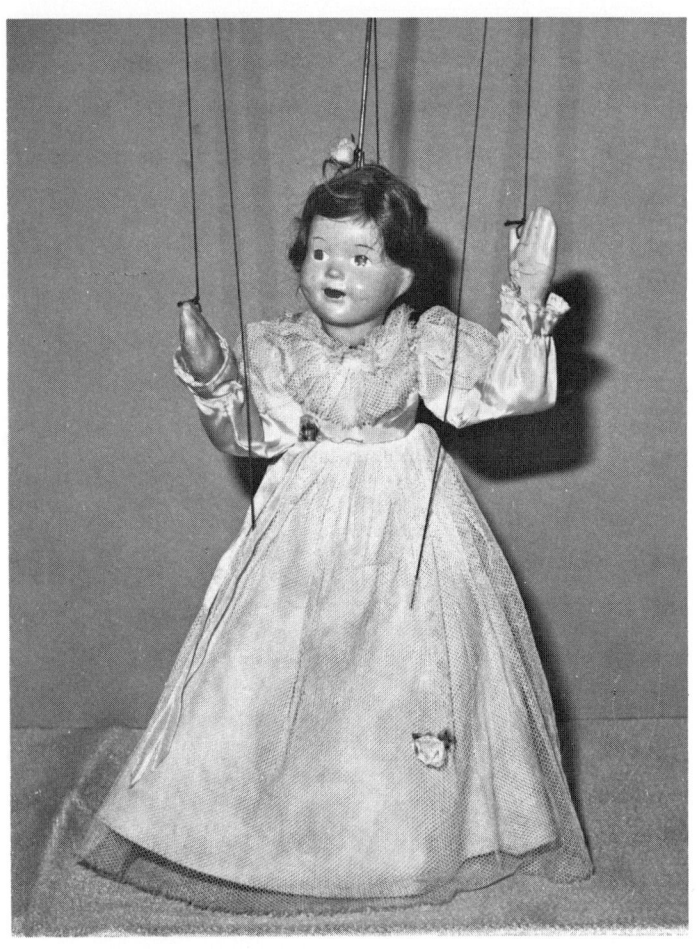

A sweet girl, this one has a smiling face with dimples. She is wearing a pink net over taffeta gown with pink rosettes on the dress and in her brown mohair wig. Perhaps this is "Princess" since she was found with the "Prince." She has no tag. (*Vivian C. Flagg Collection.*)

Although he is unmarked, this boy appears to be another "Prince" with a slightly different trim on his trousers. (*Vivian C. Flagg Collection.*)

In the May 1938 *Playthings* ad Madame Alexander introduced her marionettes of Walt Disney characters which were an exclusive arrangement with the Disney studios. They included Mickey and Minnie Mouse, Donald Duck, Pluto, Snow White and the Seven Dwarfs. They had the same body construction as the Sarg marionettes.

These two 8in. (20.3cm) characters are a mystery, but they have the same construction and string movement as the Sarg marionettes. The man has a character face with a long nose and bald head. He is wearing a blue tunic, white pants and a red and white tie. The lady is also a character with a full face and pointed chin. Her wig is red mohair. She is wearing an orange blouse, a red apron and a green skirt. (*Vivian C. Flagg Collection.*)

III. Composition Dolls
Dionne Quintuplets

The whole world marveled over the birth of the Dionne Quintuplets, five identical baby girls, in a small farmhouse near Callendar, Ontario, Canada, on the morning of May 28, 1934. And, of course, the fact that the babies survived was a miracle in itself, premature and tiny as they were with a combined weight of just over ten pounds. Nevertheless, nearly everyone loves babies, and the idea of five baby girls all alike was irresistible. The desire of the public for news of the tiny girls seemed insatiable as daily bulletins and multitudes of photographs were issued.

Of course, such a phenomenon was also big business. Crowds flocked to see the babies in their special new home just across the street from their birthplace, and of course, to buy all types of souvenirs including spoons, dishes, pennants, charms, handkerchiefs, clocks, lamps and so forth. Large companies, such as Quaker Oats and Karo, featured the Quints in ads. They were the subject of newsreels, motion pictures, books, coloring books, paper dolls, calendars and fans. Magazines featured the Quints on their covers with companion articles inside.

With all of the undeniable appeal of five identical little babies, it seems natural that someone would have hit upon the idea of making them into dolls—and Madame Alexander did, receiving exclusive rights to use the Dionne name on her dolls, which were designed by Bernard Lipfert. Her trademark was registered January 30, 1936 for Quints (#374,274), Quins (#374,269), Quinties (#374,271) and The Five Babies (#374,273). Surely, she must also have registered Quintuplets, but no record appears for it.

A news release in the April 1935 *Playthings* announced that Madame Alexander had obtained exclusive permission to "reproduce the world-famous Dionne quintuplets in doll form." The article goes on: "With the usual painstaking care typical of every Madame Alexander product, the Dionne quintuplet dolls are sculptured with remarkable fidelity in the very image of these five little babies whose fame is international."

The first ads for the Dionne Quintuplet dolls which appeared in the same issue emphasized a tie-in for the Quints' first birthday and suggested that stores hold birthday parties for Quints and dolls on May 28. This was followed by several more 1935 ads. Then Alexander started using the back cover of *Playthings*, and an ad appeared for the Dionne Quintuplet dolls every month of 1936. Of course, Madame Alexander was not the only doll executive to realize the potential sales involved in five identical babies. Many companies offered imitation Quints in sets of five or simply by themselves, and everyone knew who they represented even though these companies could not use the Dionne name. Apparently Alexander was plagued with an infringement problem as their ads stressed that Alexander was "the only firm with any authority to use the names and likenesses of these chidren, in the manufacture and sale of dolls" by authority of the legal guardians of the Quints.

The Quints were a bonanza for Alexander and certainly their first big success, probably eclipsed at the time only by Ideal's "Shirley Temple." In the January 1937 *Playthings*, the Alexander ad stated that over one million girls had one or more of the Quint dolls.

The Quintuplet dolls were manufactured by Alexander in two styles—all-composition or cloth bodies with composition heads and limbs. Each style was available in a variety of sizes and choice of clothing. It is probable that the Quintuplets, the Tony Sarg Marionettes and the small storybook and international dolls were the first composition dolls actually manufactured by the Alexander Doll Company. It appears that their earlier composition dolls were probably manufactured for them by some other doll company.

The Quintuplet dolls appeared in 1935 as babies. In 1936 toddlers with chubby straight legs were added. As the real Quints continued to grow, so did the doll series with additional models having child rather than baby faces. By 1937 the dolls were presented as children with more mature faces and even straighter and thinner legs. However, babies and early toddlers continued to be popular also. Sizes varied from the small 7-1/2in. (19.1cm) all-composition baby which sold for about $1.00 to the large 23in. (58.4cm) baby which sold for about $6.00, depending upon the costume. The Quint dolls were offered through 1939.

In the August 1936 *Playthings*, Madame Alexander announced that the company had created a complete line of all types of clothing including hats and coats for all sizes of the Dionne Quintuplet dolls. Alexander doll clothes have always been beautifully designed and well made with attention to detail, as well as durability, and the Quintuplet designs in a variety of play and dress clothes helped to establish these trends.

The dolls are marked DIONNE//ALEXANDER or just ALEXANDER. The clothes are usually tagged, although sometimes are not. The labels vary somewhat. Tag in a set of 7-1/2in. (19.1cm) toddlers:
GENUINE
DIONNE QUINTUPLET DOLLS
ALL RIGHTS RESERVED
MADAME ALEXANDER, N. Y.

Tag in a set of 7-1/2in. (19.1cm) babies:
DIONNE QUINTUPLET
(Her name)
EXCLUSIVE LICENSEE
MADAM ALEXANDER DOLL CO. [sic]

Tag on a 16in. (40.6cm) toddler:
DIONNE QUINTUPLET
MADAME ALEXANDER
NEW YORK

Tag on a 23in. (58.4cm) baby: MADAME ALEXANDER NEW YORK

Individual colors signified the specific name of the doll, as all five girls were made from the same mold. Yvonne—pink; Annette—yellow; Cecile—green; Emilie or Emelie—lavender; Marie—blue.

Some of the dolls were issued with bibs embroidered with the baby's name in her specific color to identify her. This seems to have been the first method of identification; then small gold bar pins with a hanging circle with the child's name were used. Bibs and pins can be seen in the photographs.

This set of 7-1/2in. (19.1cm) Dionne babies is like one advertised in Montgomery Ward's 1935 Christmas catalog for 79 cents each! They are all of composition with bent legs, painted eyes and straight molded hair. Their dresses are identical white organdy with the name bibs in each Quint's color to identify them individually. They are each in original labeled boxes. (*Barbara Crescenze Collection.*)

Apparently one of the first Quints, this is "Emelie," a 23in. (58.4cm) baby showing her pearly teeth. She has brown-painted straight hair and lashed brown sleep eyes. Her body is cloth with a composition swivel head on a shoulder plate, full composition arms and nearly full composition bent legs. Her hat is missing and her bib is a replacement. She is wearing her white organdy dress with puff sleeves just like she appeared in the Montgomery Ward's 1935 Christmas catalog. Her price was $4.39. The dolls of 1935 apparently did not have pins. All are pictured wearing white dresses with their names embroidered on their bibs. (*Childhood doll of Barbara Crescenze.*)

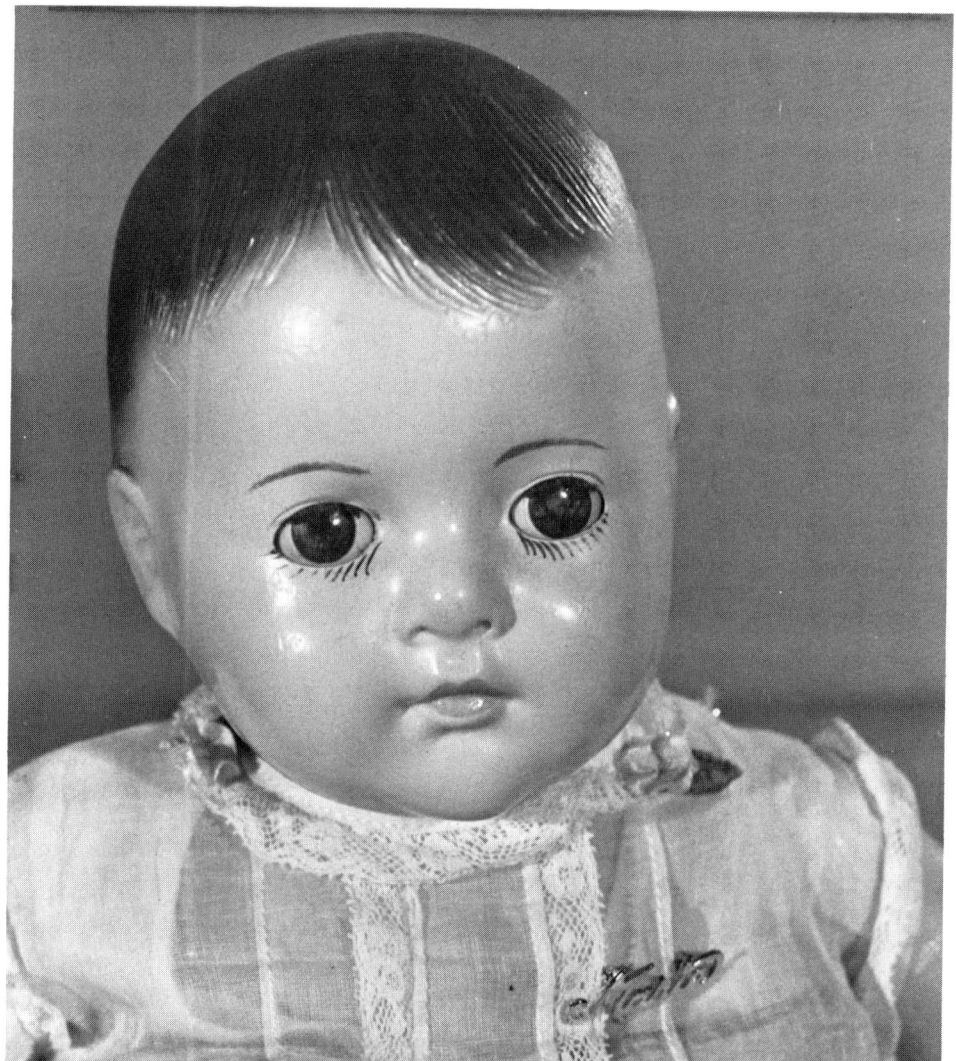

This is a close-up view of a 16in. (40.6 cm) Dionne baby with a cloth body and composition limbs. She has brown molded and painted straight hair and brown sleeping eyes. Of course, all of the Dionne Quintuplet dolls have brown hair and brown eyes, as did the real Dionnes. Her dress is probably a replacement. (*H & J Foulke.*)

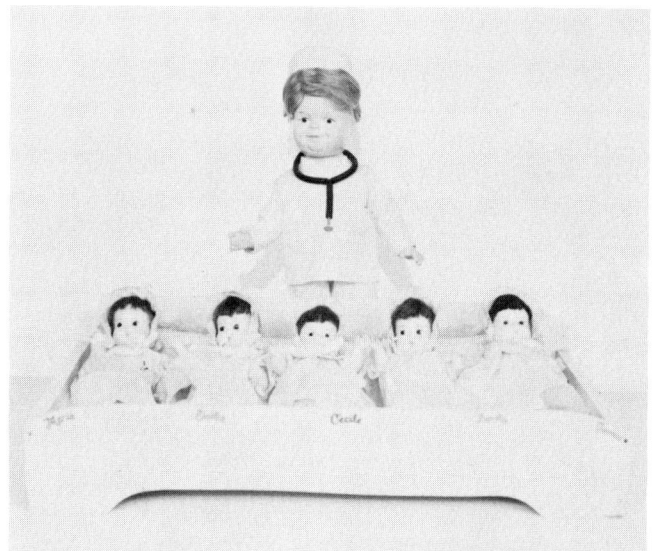

This set of 7-1/2in. (19.1cm) Quint babies with brown wigs are sleeping in a white wooden crib with individual names on it. They are attended by a 14in. (35.6cm) all-composition doctor doll, usually referred to as Dr. Dafoe, the Quints' doctor and one of their legal guardians. The doll was not advertised as Dr. Dafoe, but simply as a doctor doll for the Quints. He is unmarked, but his clothes are tagged "Madame Alexander" and consist of a white cotton doctor's uniform — pants, tunic and cap. The doll has a very interesting character face with painted eyes and a gray mohair wig. A nurse doll for the Quintuplets is pictured on page 25. (*Maxine Salaman Collection.*)

This set of 8in. (20.3cm) Quint toddlers has brown wigs. They are wearing their pins and organdy dresses with matching hats in each girl's color. Several pieces of furniture were available for the Quints including a playpen, highchair, low chair, scooter chair, bed, Quint-o-bile, basket, swing and Ferris wheel. A September 1936 Alexander ad in *Toys and Novelties* featured a merry-go-round display item for dealers who sold the Dionne Quintuplet dolls. (*Maxine Salaman Collection.*)

This set of 8in. (20.3cm) toddlers with molded curly hair and brown painted eyes is from about 1936. These little girls are wearing organdy dresses and matching hats in their own colors. They have rayon socks and snap shoes. Each also has her name pin. The booklet shown accompanied each doll and contained a poem about and a description of each Dionne girl. (*Barbara Crescenze Collection.*)

The matching set of 12in. (30.5cm) composition Dionne toddlers is wearing organdy dresses with matching hats in the appropriate colors. They have molded curly brown hair, sleeping eyes and closed mouths. All are wearing their name pins. The heads and bodies are marked "ALEXANDER." The clothes are labeled "Genuine//Dionne Quintuplet Dolls//Madame Alexander." (*Virginia Ann Heyerdahl Collection.*)

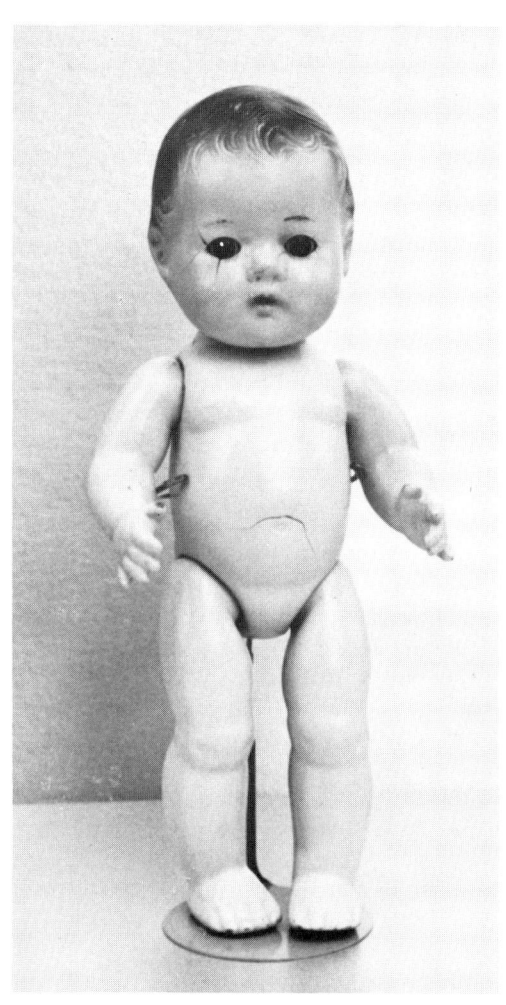

Above: An 11-1/2in. (29.2cm) Dionne toddler with curly molded hair. She is marked "ALEXANDER." (*H & J Foulke.*)

Above right: These two 11in. (27.9cm) all-composition toddlers have brown human hair wigs and brown sleeping eyes. Their legs are chubby with fat rolls at the knees, and their hands are chubby with expressive fingers. The standing girl wearing blue is "Marie," while "Annette" is sitting wearing a yellow dress. (*Barbara Crescenze Collection.*)

This all-compositon toddler is 16in. (40.6cm) tall. She has molded and painted curly brown hair with swirls on her forehead and above each ear. She is wearing a white dotted swiss dress with a lavender ribbon to indicate that this is "Emelie." She is also shown in a close-up photograph wearing her matching bonnet. (*Barbara Crescenze Collection.*)

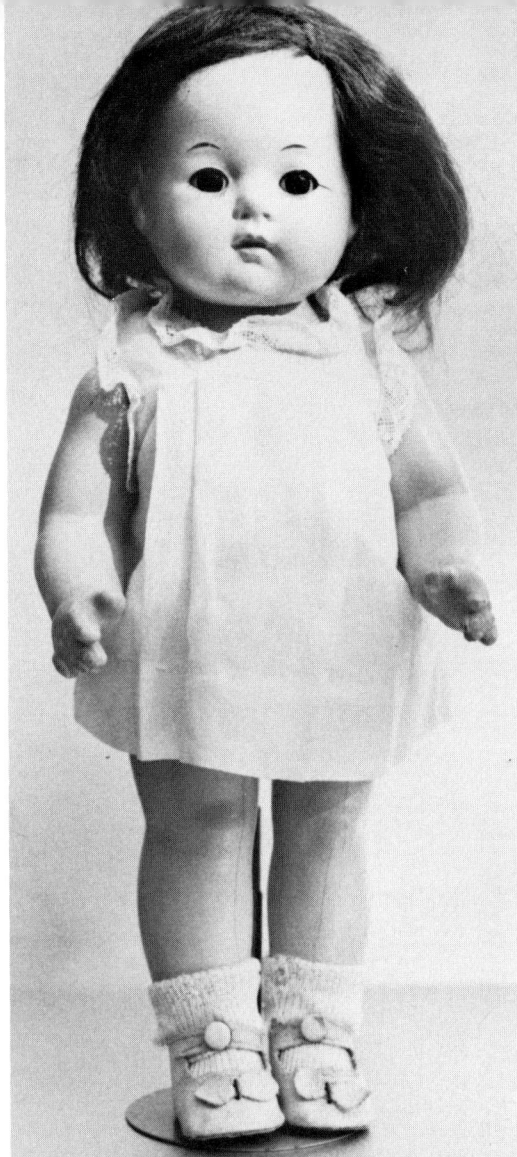

As the Dionne girls grew up, the Alexander Doll Company also produced "growing up" models of the Dionne children. This 13-1/2in. (34.3cm) girl is probably from 1937 and has the thinner legs. Her head swivels on a shoulder plate; the arms and legs are of composition; torso is cloth with a cry box inside. Her brown hair was originally curled with a ribbon bandeau and rosettes. Her footwear is original, but the originality of her untagged dress is questionable. (H & J Foulke.)

Shown in the color section on page 56, this matching set of 17in. (43.2cm) all-composition toddlers is a rarity to find since most little girls of the 1930s would not have had five of these large dolls which probably sold for about $6.00 each. They have lovely brown human hair wigs, so advertised by a gold tag on their dresses. They have sleeping eyes and open mouths with teeth showing. Their organdy dresses and hats are in the appropriate color for each Quint. The rayon sock rims have colors matching the dresses. Each of these little girls has her name pin and wrist booklet. They are marked ALEXANDER on their torsos, but their wigs are glued down too tightly to see if the heads are marked. Their clothing is labeled:
GENUINE
DIONNE QUINTUPLET DOLL
All Rights Reserved
Madame Alexander
(Maxine Salaman Collection.)

The booklet accompanying each doll contained a poem and brief description for each child which is quoted below.

YVONNE
Yvonne is cute and likes to play,
Her eyes a-twinkle, bright and gay
She flirts with everybody now.
An Actress she will be—and how!

An imp who mimics everyone and wrinkles her nose before all of her sisters to be sure that she is noticed—that is Yvonne. Now she makes faces with everyone including dear old Doctor Dafoe and her nurses if she can get them to play her game. Imitating her friends helped her with dancing. She learned to follow her instructor with the finest of dance steps.

ANNETTE
A pretty baby is Annette—
The dearest one you've ever met.
She always likes to sing and croon.
Perhaps she'll be a "star" real soon.

This little lady likes to find out all about things and loves to have people give her their whole attention. She wants her prettiness to be appreciated. Once she cried, so that people would listen just to her. She found they paid less attention to her than when she was good, so she stopped. She knows everyone loves her and is not afraid of anything.

EMELIE
Emelie is the active one,
She twists and tumbles just for fun.
And in her bath she loves to play
A swimmer she should be some day.

Here is the liveliest girl of a lively crew. She likes to dance with her hands waving over her head. She delights in playing motorman on the special Dionne Toy train. When anyone suggests play, Emelie may be found laughing and running in the very middle of it. Of course her kiddie car is fun and she found that out real soon. Now she is the speediest Quin.

CECILE
Cecile would make a lovely prize.
She's very brave and seldom cries.
She seems to say, "Things could be worse!"
When she grows up, she'll be a nurse.

A quiet peaceful girl who is happy every day, all day long and never finds it hard to play by herself. One year and a half ago when she was very young, she heard a shade making a great noise and woke up to find it was very dark; but nothing touched her so she turned over and went to sleep. Very few other girls at 6 months could be so brave.

MARIE
Now here's a darling one—Marie.
She seldom makes a sound you see.
In fact she's such a peaceful one
It's likely she'll be lots of fun.

Little Marie likes her bright toys and gay shining dishes. She likes to sit apart and enjoy the things she watches. She is very insistent when she wants anything and usually gets it. She never follows suit unless her sisters have all gone before.

The Small Composition Dolls

It appears that some of the first composition dolls actually manufactured by Alexander are the small 7in. (17.8cm) and 9in. (22.9cm) ones that are very often overlooked by collectors. These little dolls came in darling costumes and in a wide variety of over 50 characters. They were made from about 1935 until about 1943.

The face on the 7in. (17.8cm) composition doll has a cute pointed chin, pug nose and painted eyes looking to the side. Although a variety of storybook and international costumes were used, the faces were all the same mold, with some variation in coloring and decoration.

The 9in. (22.9cm) size doll was probably made from 1937 to about 1943. Like the 7in. (17.8cm) size, this face, which is long and slender but with a more rounded chin, was used for a wide variety of sweet little girls and storybook characters as well as children in ethnic costume. The 9in. (22.9cm) size also has painted eyes. It appears that this was the first use of the name "Wendy Ann" who was a popular little girl in the series. The dolls are marked on their torsos either "MME ALEXANDER" or:

WENDY ANN
MME ALEXANDER

This 7in. (17.8cm) doll is labeled "Finnish." She has blonde wavy mohair and a red and white costume with apron and matching cap. This 7in. (17.8cm) size doll has painted shoes and socks. She is marked "MME ALEXANDER" on her torso. (*H & J Foulke.*)

Above right: This 9in. (22.9cm) all-composition little girl is tagged "McGuffey Ana." She is wearing a blue flowered cotton dress with white organdy pinafore and white organdy dust cap with flower trim. Her wig is of blonde mohair with pigtails, and her brown eyes are painted to the side. The blonde wig with curly bangs and braids is a trademark of "McGuffey Ana." For a "McGuffey Ana" in a larger size composition doll see page 26. (*H & J Foulke.*)

Above left: Typical of the series of 9in. (22.9cm) international and storybook dolls released in the late 1930s is this pair with blonde mohair and eyes painted to the side. The boy is wearing a green felt suit and matching hat; the girl wears a dress with a yellow skirt, dark bodice and white apron. They have lost their tags, but appear to be the "Swiss" girl and boy. (*Barbara Crescenze Collection.*)

Betty Face

This 13in. (33cm) "Little Colonel" is exactly as shown in Montgomery Ward's 1935 catalog. She was offered for $1.98. She is wearing a pink organdy above-the-knee party dress trimmed with matching net and satin streamers. Her poke bonnet matches her dress. The blonde mohair wig has soft curls; her eyes are brown. (*H & J Foulke.*)

It has become the custom among Alexander doll collectors to refer to the various doll faces by either the name of the doll who was first given that particular face or the name of the doll who was most often found with that face. Although Alexander doll history of the early 1930s is a little fuzzy, this face has traditionally been called "Little Betty," shortened here to simply "Betty." The distinguishing characteristics of the "Betty" face are two tiny dimples, one each side of her closed mouth.

The most sought after dolls with the "Betty" face are the "Little Colonel" dolls, based on Annie Fellows Johnston's books about a "vivacious Kentucky bred child" of Civil War days. They were presented in the March 1935 *Playthings*. Since Ideal Novelty & Toy Company had the rights to Shirley Temple, who was the star of the film, and to her film outfits, Alexander could not mention the popular child star in their ads, but did advertise a tie-in with both the film and the book.

The Alexander "Little Colonel" dolls came in a variety of the beautifully designed and executed costumes for which Madame Alexander was becoming well-known. Some of them were authentic Civil War period costumes with pantalettes and others were in modern little girl styles. The dolls came in three sizes: 13in. (33cm), 17in. (43.2cm) and 22in. (55.9cm). The 13in. (33cm) size used the "Betty" face with closed mouth and dimples. Although the ads stated blonde mohair wigs, some dolls did come with brown. The larger sizes of the "Little Colonel" used a face with an open smiling mouth. From ads it appears that most of these larger dolls had long blonde mohair curls, but some had shorter hair with bangs. Clothing labels vary on this series, some saying "Little Colonel," some saying simply "Madam Alexander." The latter provides an identification problem as to whether a doll is actually "Little Betty" or the "Little Colonel."

Another 13in. (33cm) "Little Colonel" is wearing a period costume. Her organdy dress has ruffles at the armhole and waist as well as three rows of ruffles at the hem of her just-above-the-ankle skirt. Pantalettes peek out from under her dress. Her matching bonnet is trimmed with ruffles and a tiny bouquet of flowers. She has a dark mohair wig styled with bangs. (*Rosemary Dent Collection.*)

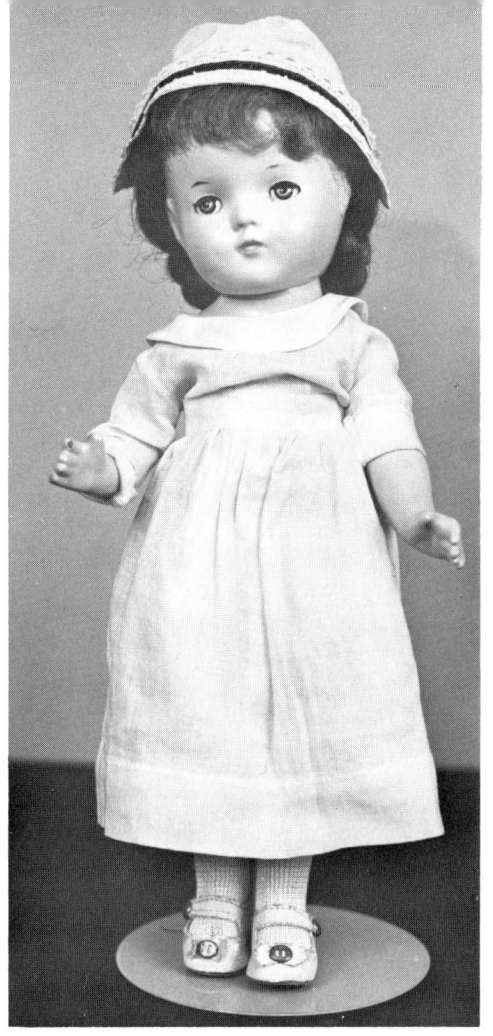

This 13in. (33cm) nurse doll was created to go along with the Dionne Quintuplet dolls. The real Quints' nurse was Yvonne Leroux who in late 1936 made a promotional tour for Madame Alexander and the Quint dolls. Her just above-the-ankle dress is of white cotton, and she has white stockings and white strap shoes. (*Maxine Salaman Collection.*)

The "Betty" face was also used for this 13in. (33cm) version of "Princess Elizabeth." Here she is wearing her blue taffeta gown and gold tiara with the crown center, completely attired for her father's coronation. Her hair is blonde; her eyes are blue. The wrist tag is original, and her clothing is tagged "Princess Elizabeth." A different version of the "Princess Elizabeth" doll is shown below. (*H & J Foulke.*)

Princess Elizabeth Face

"Princess Elizabeth" was designed for the May 12, 1937 coronation of her father, George VI, King of England. She had a new smiling face with open mouth and upper teeth. She was assured of success since every little girl at sometime or another imagines herself a real princess. "Princess Elizabeth" came in a variety of gowns. She wore a tiara with a crown in the center or headpiece of sequins. Maxine Salaman also has her dressed in a short tagged yellow everyday dress with matching tagged coat and hat.

In this photo "Princess Elizabeth" is wearing a gown of dusty rose organdy with a ruffle flounce and white lace and black ribbon trim. Her blonde human hair wig is side-parted with low blonde curls. Her clothing is labeled "Princess Elizabeth." She is 13in. (33cm) tall, but also came in 16in. (40.6cm), 18in. (45.7cm), 20in. (50.8cm) and 24in. (61cm) sizes. Usually she is marked on the back of her head:
PRINCESS ELIZABETH
ALEXANDER DOLL CO.
(*Maxine Salaman Collection.*)

As noted in the beginning chapter, sometimes the Alexander dolls are not marked at all. The "Princess Elizabeth" doll presents another peculiarity in that sometimes the 13in. (33cm) size is marked on the torso simply 13, whereas the head could be unmarked or be marked ⊕. "Princess Elizabeth" also came in a version with the "Betty" face pictured on the previous page.

The "Princess Elizabeth" face was used for quite a few other dolls, and although they are different characters, their heads carry the PRINCESS ELIZABETH mark. The hair style and clothing and wrist tags are very important in identifying these girls. The one found most frequently is "McGuffey Ana" also issued in 1937. (Sometimes her name is spelled without the "e" or with a hyphen.) She was designed to be an old-fashioned schoolgirl reminiscent of the days of the little red schoolhouse where the famous McGuffey Readers were used. Hence, her name came from the famous old readers. She was a popular doll and production was fairly consistent from 1937 to 1944, in composition. She came in every size from 9in. (22.9 cm) to 24in. (61cm). The 9in. (22.9cm) size is shown on page 23. "McGuffey Ana" has been an Alexander favorite since her conception in 1937 and has also been produced in hard plastic and vinyl. See pages 46 and 76 for two other variations.

This is the 20in. (50.8cm) doll as she appeared in several large *Playthings* ads. She has a red plaid dress topped by a white organdy apron with ruffles over the shoulder. Her hair style nearly always has blonde pigtails and curly bangs. She also wears her high button shoes. Some dolls came with a straw hat; some did not. The wrist tag on this doll is interesting as it shows her in front of a schoolhouse. It says: "I am McGuffey-Ana and Madame Alexander has made me look like my mommie did when she went to school. I hope I will make you very happy." Her clothing is tagged "McGuffey Ana." (*Rosemary Dent Collection.*)

This "McGuffey Ana" is the hard-to-find 11in. (27.9cm) size. Here she appears to be a closed-mouth version of the "Princess Elizabeth" mold. She wears a blue print dress covered by a white organdy apron with lace on the pocket and over the shoulder. These small sizes usually wore a ruffled organdy dust cap with flower trim and low snap shoes, the ones here being replacements. Her clothing is tagged "McGuffey Ana." (*Edna Black Collection.*)

Right: This 16in. (40.6cm) "McGuffey Ana" is dressed in an unusual style for her. She is wearing a Kate Greenaway style ivory silk dress with a high waist and puffed short sleeves. The trim is green chiffon ruffles. Her bonnet has a wide brim with a flower bouquet at the side. She has the typical pigtails, brown eyes and high button shoes. Her clothing is tagged "McGuffey Ana." (*Maxine Salaman Collection.*)

Left: This 13in. (33cm) doll wears a red and white checked cotton dress with a white organdy pinafore. She has a red straw hat and red high snap shoes. Her hair is the typical blonde pigtails with curly bangs. The "McGuffey Ana" school dresses came in a wide variety of plaids and prints. She has lost her clothing label, but has her original wrist tag. (*Barbara Crescenze Collection.*)

"Flora McFlimsey of Madison Square" is the clothes label on this 13in. (33cm) doll. Another use of the "Princess Elizabeth" mold, this time with red human hair and freckles, she was made during the 1938-1944 period. Since she is too early to be based on the Mariana books, possibly she is based on the 1857 poem "Nothing to Wear" by W.A. Butler. She is wearing a green cotton dress with a green and white checked pinafore, brown high snap shoes and a green straw hat. Her wrist tag is original but the hatbox is not. "Flora McFlimsey" is always dressed in old-fashioned style. (*Beth Foulke Collection.*)

Mr. Butler's poem is a very long poem, but is starts out:
"Miss Flora McFlimsey, of Madison Square,
Has made three separate journeys to Paris,
And her father assures me, each time she was there,
That she and her friend Mrs. Harris...
Spent six consecutive weeks without stopping
In one continuous round of shopping."

It continues:
"And yet, though scarce three months have passed since the day
This merchandise went, on twelve carts up Broadway,
This same Miss McFlimsey, of Madison Square,
The last time we met was in utter despair,
Because she had nothing whatever to wear!"
(The poem goes on for seven more pages about her lack of attire!)

"Snow White" was the rage in 1938, and as a tie-in with the Walt Disney film, dominated the toy trade journals. Along with Ideal and Knickerbocker, Madame Alexander was licensed to produce "Snow White" dolls. The Alexander "Snow White" was made from 1937-1939 using a closed-mouth version of the "Princess Elizabeth" mold.

Another use of the "Princess Elizabeth" mold was for the "Kate Greenaway" doll which was produced from 1938-1943. She wore a period-type costume from the Kate Greenaway drawings so popular in the 1880s but reflecting the styles of the early 1800s. "Kate Greenaway" has a bright yellow or blonde mohair wig with bangs and side and back curls. In the 1942-1943 catalog, she is listed in 13in. (33cm), 15in. (38.1cm), 16in. (40.6cm) 20in. (50.8cm) and 24in. (61cm) sizes.

This 13in. (33cm) Snow White" wears a labeled dress with pink taffeta skirt and sleeves and a blue velvet bodice. Her cape is blue taffeta. She nearly always has black hair and brown eyes. Usually the face color is very pale, but this particular doll has very pretty cheek color. A distinctive feature is the "Snow White" slippers with tiny heels, turned up toes and tiny bows. Dresses came in several pastel colors. The dress pictured also came in yellow with a bronze bodice. Another style featured a net overskirt. Sizes advertised were 13in. (33cm) and 17in. (43.2cm), but the smallest is the most commonly found. The 13in. (33cm) size also came with painted eyes. (*Vivian C. Flagg Collection.*)

This 20in. (50.8cm) "Kate Greenaway" is wearing a pink chiffon dress with a scalloped hem, lace edging and blue trim. A corsage of flowers at the waist and blue wristlets accent her dress which is styled with a high waist and puffy sleeves. A large brimmed hat with a feather accent completes the ensemble. Her clothing is labeled "Kate Greenaway." (*Maxine Salaman Collection.*)

This 16in. (40.6cm) "Kate Greenaway" is just as she appears in the 1942-1943 catalog. She is wearing a blue organdy dress with a striped flower print fabric for contrast at hem, sleeves and waist. She wears blue lace wristlets and carries a blue organdy reticule. Her bonnet is of blue velvet. Her dress is labeled "Kate Greenaway." (*Edna Black Collection.*)

Here is a close-up view of a 15in. (38.1cm) "Kate Greenaway" dressed in pale pink organdy with a very fancy matching hat. She has a typical blonde mohair wig, and is shown in the 1942-1943 catalog. Her clothing is labeled "Kate Greenaway." (*Maxine Salaman Collection.*)

Wendy Ann Face

The "Wendy Ann" face apparently was in use as early as 1936 or 1937, although the doll herself was not widely promoted until the September 1938 ad in *Playthings*. Even after the "Wendy Ann" doll was discontinued in about 1940, the face continued to be used until the switch from composition to hard plastics in 1947 and 1948. The face is a very appealing one with pointed chin, closed rosebud mouth and somber expression. The body construction is interesting also. The arms are molded differently: the right is bent at the elbow; the left extends gracefully. The doll swivels at the waist, and has a hip joint which allows her to bend forward. A news release in the October 1938 *Playthings* described "Wendy Ann" as modeled like any little girl of seven or eight years old, with a slender body and long thin arms and legs. ("Wendy Ann" was named for Madame Alexander's own granddaughter.) She could be put into at least 12 different positions: she could touch her toes, swing her arms over her head, recline on her elbow, sit up, stand up, bend backwards and forwards. She came only in the 13-14in. (33-35.6cm) size. There was also a 9in. (22.9cm) doll called "Wendy Ann" who had the sweet composition face with painted eyes shown on page 23. A hard plastic "Wendy Ann" in 15in. (38.1cm) and 18in. (45.7 cm) sizes with a "Margaret" face was made in 1948 and 1949.

Marks on head: ALEXANDER
Marks on body (this is on the 9in. (22.9cm) and 13-14in. (33-35.6cm): WENDY-ANN
 ALEXANDER
(Many of these models are not marked at all.)

Right: Here is "Wendy Ann" in the most usual version with a dark blonde human hair wig and sleeping eyes. She is wearing white jodhpurs and a blouse with a black weskit and cap. Very stunning indeed! Her clothing is labeled "Wendy Ann." (*Maxine Salaman Collection.*)

Left: This 14in. (35.6cm) "Wendy Ann" is the rare form with the molded brown hair and blue painted eyes. Her light blue dress with full skirt, puff sleeves and square neckline was a popular Alexander style. It is trimmed with navy blue ribbon. She is wearing an attractive navy blue hat. Her clothing is labeled "Wendy Ann." (*Maxine Salaman Collection.*)

This close-up of "Wendy Ann" shows her dark blonde human hair wig with curls across her forehead and longer curls at the sides and back of her hair. She has brown eyes. Her pink party dress has lace trim with a black velvet ribbon sash and bow on her pink straw hat. She also has black lace wristlets which do not show in the photo. Her clothing is labeled "Wendy Ann." (*Barbara Crescenze Collection.*)

"Madelaine du Baine" has generally been considered an exclusive for F.A.O. Schwarz during 1937-1939. Supposedly Alexander made an entirely different "Madelaine" in 1940 which causes some confusion about these dolls. However, the photo which Louella Hart used with this latter notation in her *Spinning Wheel* article is actually a hard plastic "McGuffey Ana" not a "Madelaine." But Alexander does have a trademark of May 1940 #431,900 for a "Madelaine." The problem of tags do not help either as it seems "Madelaine" and "Madelaine du Bain" (also spelled de Baine and du Baine) were used interchangeably on dolls with the same or nearly the same costumes. In the February 1941 *Playthings* ad Alexander listed a "Madelaine De Baine" with their regular line. Perhaps F.A.O. Schwarz had an exclusive for a year or so before general distribution of this doll, or perhaps they had an exclusive on only one costume or size. There are endless possibilities to this riddle. Anyway, "Madelaine" came in a variety of sizes and costume variations.

Above: This 11in. (27.9cm) "Madelaine du Bain" is wearing a blue skirt with pink printed roses. The ruffle around the skirt edge has a row of pink rickrack at the top. Her bodice is pink organdy with sleeve ruffles to match the skirt. Her fancy lace hat has flower trim. Some of the "Madelaines" had long organdy pantaloons and some had only knee-length ones. (*Maxine Salaman Collection.*)

Right: Here is the 21in. (53.3cm) "Fairy Princess" as she appears in Alexander's 1942-1943 "Album of Dolls." She was offered in 11in. (27.9cm), 15in. (38.1cm), 18in. (45.7cm) and 22in. (55.9cm) sizes. Her long dress is of gold satin with a net front panel edged with embroidered lace. Her long wavy blonde human hair is crowned by a sequin tiara. She is wearing a long gold beaded necklace. Her clothing is labeled "Fairy Princess." (*Helen Teske Collection.*)

Above left: This 14in. (35.6cm) doll with the "Wendy Ann" face is certainly puzzling as she is tagged "Princess Elizabeth" but is wearing the "Fairy Princess" costume! She has long blonde human hair in shoulder length topped by a tiara of gold sequins. Her pink taffeta dress has a full paneled skirt, alternate panels having gold circles, as do her sleeves. Her long gold beaded necklace is original. She is probably from the 1940-1943 period. (*Maxine Salaman Collection.*)

Left: Brides and their attendants have always been included in the Alexander line. In the mid-1940s whole bridal parties were available. This 21in. (53.3cm) "Bridesmaid" is wearing a blue satin gown with a gathered waist, a square neckline and long sleeves. In place of a bouquet, she is carrying a blue satin muff with flower trim. She has a flower headpiece on her blonde mohair wig. Her dress is tagged "Madame Alexander." (*H & J Foulke.*)

Above right: A special doll for the World War II years was this 14in. (35.6cm) "Miss America." Her hand is molded in a clenched position with a hole in the middle to hold the flag. She is wearing a military style hat, a red and white striped dress and red snap shoes. Her long curls are blonde and her eyes are brown. She is probably from 1944. Her dress is tagged "Miss America." (*Maxine Salaman Collection.*)

One of the twelve special portrait dolls of 1946 is this 21in. (53.3cm) "Judy" as shown in the November 1946 *Playthings* ad. She wears a blue taffeta gown flaring very full from the waist. Pink-pleated trim with blue edging forms the sleeves and there are large swirls of decoration at the hem of the skirt. Tiny blue artificial flowers adorn her hair, bodice and hem swirls. She is wearing nail polish and eye shadow. Her brown mohair wig is pulled up at the sides into large rolls and is long in the back and slightly curled. There is a flower decoration across the top of her hair. She is wearing her green cloverleaf wrist tag and her clothing has a "Madame Alexander" tag. (Helen Teske Collection.)

This 14in. (35.6cm) "Alice in Wonderland" uses the swivel waist "Wendy Ann" body. Her dress is blue cotton with white squares and trim. The white organdy pinafore has eyelet ruffles around the edge. Although blonde, her hair is not in the usual style as on other small "Alices." Her clothing is tagged "Alice in Wonderland." She probably dates from 1946 and 1947. The Wendy-faced "Alice" also came in a 17in. (43.2 cm) size with the same print dress. See page 35 for a different composition "Alice in Wonderland" using the "Margaret" face. (Edna Black Collection.)

Margaret Face

Margaret O'Brien was a child star of many popular movies, including *Meet Me in St. Louis* and *Little Women*. The "Margaret O'Brien" doll with the brand new face was introduced on a special June 6, 1946 TV program sponsored by Wanamaker's and featuring Madame Alexander herself. The doll was also featured in the Alexander ad in the October 1946 *Playthings*. She came in 14in. (35.6cm), 18in. (45.7cm) and 21in. (53.3cm) sizes and wore a variety of school and party dresses often with a straw hat. The wigs were with bangs and looped-up braids in various shades of brown. Her eyes were usually hazel, but did vary. "Margaret O'Brien" was made from 1946-1947 in composition. For a hard plastic version of this doll, see page 45. The dolls are sometimes marked ALEXANDER on head and/or body.

This 14in. (35.6cm) "Margaret O'Brien" has a blue cotton dress with lace trim in a pinafore outline. Puff sleeves are cuffed and edged in lace. Pink and white bows add further decoration, and her pink straw hat adds the finishing touch to her outfit. The dolls wore black or white tie or snap shoes. This doll's dress is labeled "Madame Alexander." (Edna Black Collection.)

This close-up view shows a "Margaret" face with a blonde mohair wig and gray eyes. Her corduroy coat and hat are untagged so she presents a mystery. Is she a blonde-haired "Margaret O'Brien"? Or is she a re-dressed "Gretel"? (*Joanna Ott Collection.*)

Apparently a very special set of dolls using the "Margaret" face, this composition "Hansel" and hard plastic "Gretel" are probably from 1948, the transition period from composition to hard plastic. Both of these dolls have blonde mohair wigs and blue eyes. "Gretel" is wearing a pink weskit and skirt, a blue print blouse, a white organdy apron, white stockings and black shoes. "Hansel" has light blue pants and bolero, white shirt with long sleeves and round collar and a matching red plaid stock and sash. His cap is red-striped with a tassel. He is also wearing white hose and black shoes. "Hansel" has his original "Madame Alexander" wrist tag. Both dolls have clothing labels. (*Maxine Salaman Collection.*)

This 15in. (38.1cm) "Fairy Queen" appears to be of the transition period 1947-1948, as she also came in hard plastic, which version appears on page 46. She came in at least two sizes: 15in. (38.1cm) and 18in. (45.7cm). She is wearing a tulle over taffeta dress with tulle peplum and sleeves. Gold braid trims the neckline and bodice. Flower and ribbon posies decorate the sleeves, peplum and skirt. Her hat has gold braid trim. She is carrying her "magic" wand. Some "Fairy Queen" dolls had wings. The 1947 Sears catalog shows the "Fairy Queen" with a "Wendy Ann" face. (*Edna Black Collection.*)

"Alice in Wonderland" has been in the Alexander doll line almost continuously for over 50 years. This 15in. (38.1cm) composition version has a long curled blonde mohair wig. Her blue cotton dress has a white organdy with lace trimmed pinafore. A black velvet bow trims her neckline. She has the traditional long white stockings. This doll was available in 15in. (38.1cm), 18in. (45.7cm) and 21in. (53.3 cm) sizes. A smaller size with the "Wendy Ann" face is shown on page 33. This composition doll probably dates from 1946 and 1947; the "Margaret" face was also used on a hard plastic "Alice in Wonderland" in 1948. (*Barbara Crescenze Collection.*)

In 1948 the Alexander Doll Company made the switch from composition to hard plastics. The "Margaret" mold was continued in this new medium. See pages 45 to 58 for dolls utilizing this face in hard plastic.

Individual Faces

Some of the composition dolls of the early 1930s apparently were not manufactured by Alexander, but were purchased from other companies and dressed in clothing made and designed by Alexander.

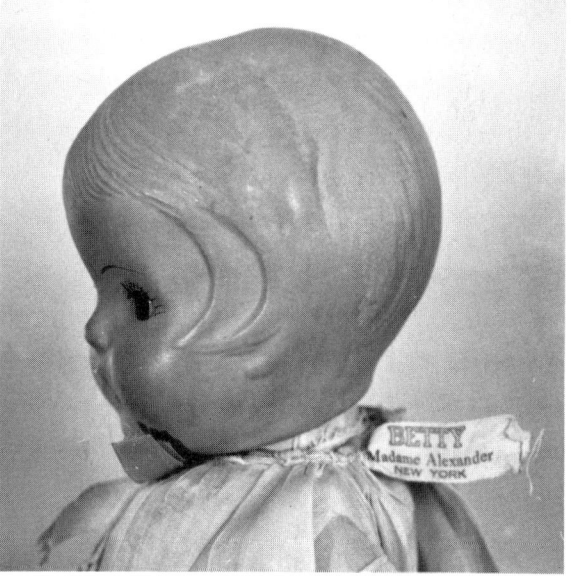

This 16in. (40.6cm) doll labeled "Betty" appears to be one of these. The doll itself is not marked. "Betty" wears a pink organdy matching dress and hat. She has molded but unpainted hair in the bobbed "Patsy" style, but this doll never had a wig, although some "Betty" dolls did. Her blue-green sleeping eyes are lashed. Her mouth is in the rosebud shape. She was purchased from the original owner. (*H & J Foulke.*)

Madame Alexander contracted in 1936 with the Withers family to make a doll of Jane who was a very popular child star of the mid-1930s. The doll was announced in the May 1936 *Playthings* on page 60. Jane Withers was billed as "The Imp of the Movies" in an Alexander promotional display poster of 1937. Her name on a marquee was sure to draw large crowds.

The "Jane Withers" doll was made in composition in 13in. (33cm), 15in. (38.1cm), 17in. (43.2 cm) and 20in. (50.8cm) sizes. Her wig was of brown human hair, and her lashed sleeping eyes were brown also. The 13in. (33cm) size had a closed mouth and more nearly resembles Jane's photo on the wrist tag than the larger doll which usually had an open mouth (although closed-mouth versions of the large doll have been reported). All of the dolls came with the gold name pin.

This 13in. (33cm) imp is wearing a dress with white dotted swiss bodice and yellow piqué cotton skirt. It has a square neck with a tatted lace yoke, puff sleeves and a full skirt. A black velvet ribbon is inserted at the waist to match her black shoes. She is wearing a matching fabric bonnet which is unusual as most "Janes" wore straw hats. There are no marks on the doll. Her dress is labeled "Madame Alexander," although some were labeled "Jane Withers." (*Rosemary Dent Collection.*)

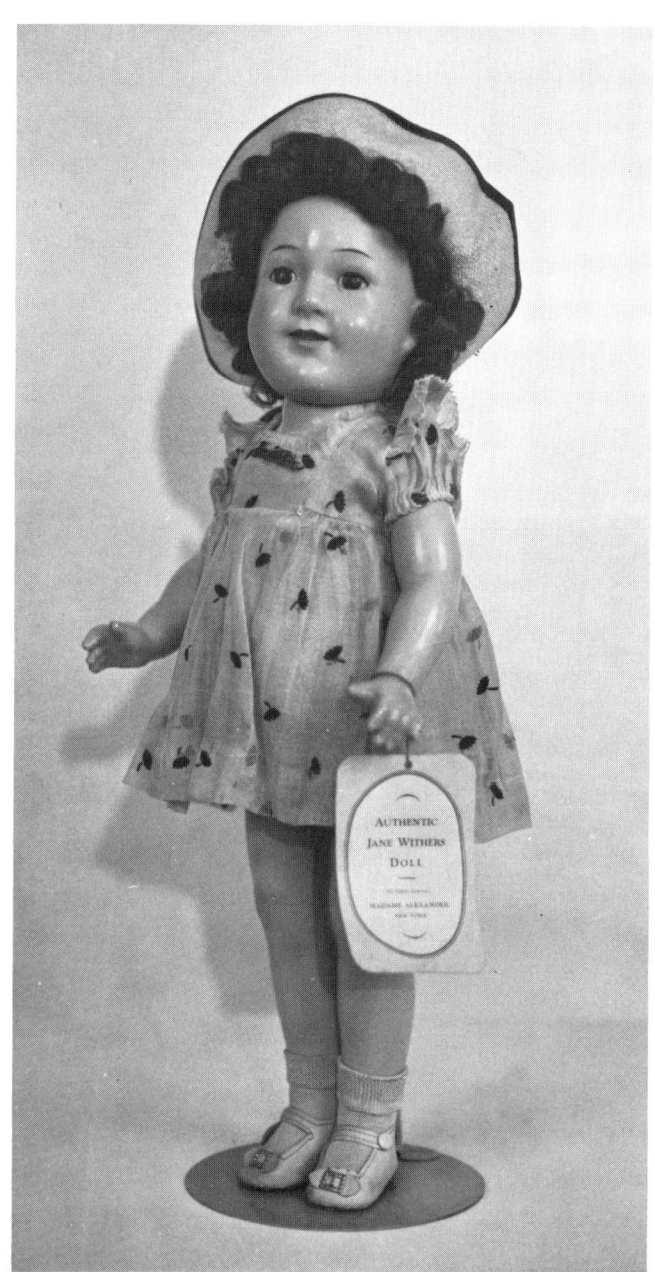

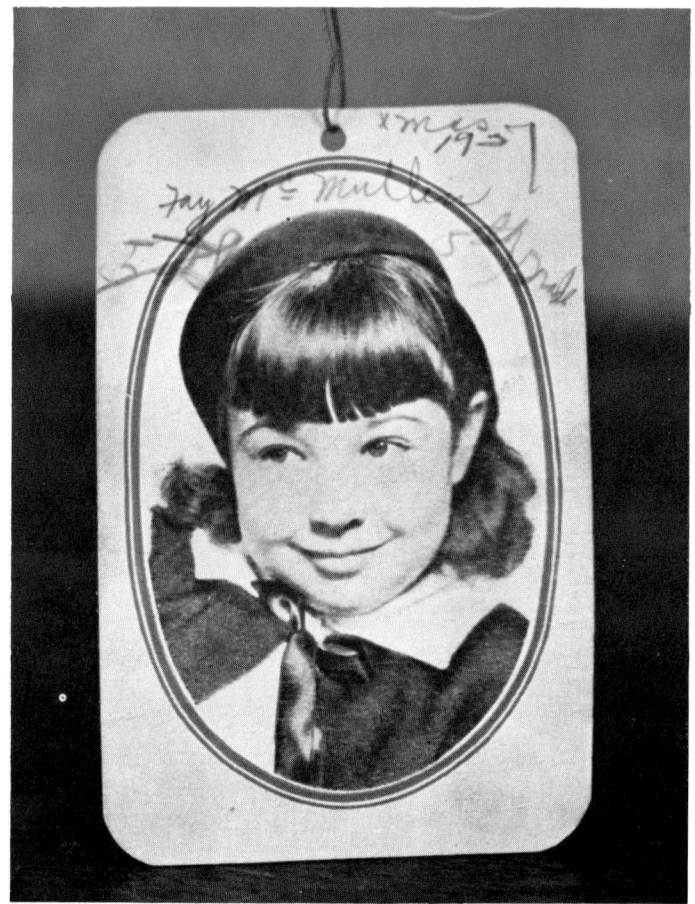

This 20in. (50.8cm) "Jane Withers" has the open mouth, brown human hair wig and brown sleeping eyes. She is not as impish looking as the 13in. (33cm) one or as the photo on the wrist tag belonging to the large doll. Lorraine Burdick reports that Jane did not like the doll because it made her look too pretty when she was actually known as an "imp" so the family cancelled the contract. Apparently then, the dolls were manufactured for only one year which accounts for their scarcity. "Jane Withers" is one of the most sought-after of the Alexander dolls. This "Jane Withers" is wearing a pink cotton dress with blue print. It has side gathers on the skirt, a square lace-edged neckline and puff sleeves with a matching ruffle. Her hat is pink straw with a blue band and her shoes and socks are white. (*Barbara Crescenze Collection.*)

Madame Alexander announced the "Sonja Henie" dolls in the April 1939 *Playthings*. They were produced until 1943, although during the last two years they were simply referred to as "Skating Dolls." A *Playthings* promotional article of November 1939 says: "In designing these winsome little doll replicas of Miss Henie, Madame Alexander has succeeded in capturing and reproducing the fresh, dainty charm of this world renowned young skater who has become the idol of American girlhood." The article also mentioned the spectacular attendance at her ice show—80,000 in one week in New York. Sonja Henie was three times an Olympic gold medalist, and made movies in addition to having her own ice revue.

The "Sonja Henie" doll is all of composition in 13in. (33cm), 15in. (38.1cm), 18in. (45.7cm) and 21in. (53.3cm) sizes, with the 13-14in. (33-35.6 cm) size sometimes appearing on the "Wendy Ann" swivel waist body. Her wigs were in several shades of light colors in either human hair or mohair. She came in a variety of skating and sports outfits and also as a bride. The doll is marked on the head MADAME ALEXANDER-SONJA HENIE or ALEXANDER or nothing.

Above: This 13in. (33cm) "Sonja Henie" is wearing a skating dress with red velvet bodice having a lace-edged square neck and puff sleeves. Her skirt is white with a red print. She wears a rosebud at her neckline and a corsage of flowers in her hair. Her dress is tagged "Sonja Henie." (*Rosemary Dent Collection.*)

Center: Another 13in. (33cm) "Sonja Henie" is wearing an original skiing outfit consisting of a red jacket and navy blue pants. The skis and poles are also original. The "Sonja Henie" doll was also available in trunk and wardrobes sets. (*Rosemary Dent Collection.*)

This 21in. (53.3cm) "Sonja Henie" is shown with her picture wrist tag. She is wearing a blue taffeta dress for skating with sequin trim and a blue organdy overskirt. Her wig is blonde human hair and she has a tiny flower hat. (*Maxine Salaman Collection.*)

A "Jeannie Walker" doll was the companion of my childhood. I wish I could remember for certain which Christmas I received her, but I think it was probably 1943. It was not until I became interested in dolls that I saw her in a book and read that she was an Alexander doll. Little girls do not necessarily pay any attention to what is written on the backs of their dolls even if it is in large capital letters! Although I did not know she was made by Alexander, I did know that she was a "Jeannie Walker" and I always called her by that name. I certainly wish I had her today, but my mother believed in keeping the attic cleaned out, so I have no idea where she is today. But if you should ever come across a 14in. (35.6cm) "Jeannie Walker" with a broken walking mechanism somewhere in New Jersey, maybe, just maybe, she was mine!

"Jeannie Walker" was advertised in *Playthings* in May 1941 as "Jeannie Walker, the Doll That Sits, Stands, and WALKS Like a Perfect Little Lady. Take her by the hand and she walks as easily and gracefully as the little girl she depicts." There is a pin that goes through her legs and bottom torso which helps her legs to walk. All of the "Jeannie Walkers" that I have seen have had brown eyes and hair, except for one which was blonde.

"Jeannie Walker" is listed in the Alexander 1942-1943 catalog as an entirely new doll, but she is not shown in the blue dress in which she is most frequently found. She came only in 14in. (35.6cm) and 18in. (45.7cm) sizes. She is marked on the body: ALEXANDER
    PAT. NO 2171281

This 14in. (35.6cm) "Jeannie Walker" is like the one I had as a child except this one has unusual blonde hair. Her dress is the same as that of the larger doll except it is a shantung cotton instead of piqué. (*Jan Foulke Collection.*)

The 18in. (45.7cm) doll pictured is the same as the one in the Alexander *Playthings* ads of May, June and September 1941. She is wearing a light blue piqué dress with a pleated skirt and high waist. Her bodice has a round collar piped in white. The sleeves are white organdy with embroidered stars and chevrons. Her natural straw hat has a blue grosgrain ribbon. The 18in. (45.7cm) doll has chubby legs with pigeon-toed feet; whereas the 14in. (35.6cm) size has thinner legs. Both sizes have a tiny closed mouth. (*Rosemary Dent Collection.*)

IV. Hard Plastic Dolls
Maggie Face

Madame Alexander made the significant change from composition to hard plastic in 1948. There would, of course, be some overlapping as old stock would be used up. The dolls were advertised as made of a rosy lightweight plastic, virtually unbreakable. Some of the dolls do have a creamy complexion, while others look suntanned.

The first new face which was created for the new medium was an appealing one with high forehead, round eyes and chubby cheeks. Collectors have come to refer to this face as "Maggie" although "Maggie" herself as a doll may not have been made until 1949. The dating on her creation as a doll is not certain, although it is known that "Maggie" was made until 1953 with the face continuing to be used until 1956. Sometimes she had the walking mechanism, in which case she would properly be referred to as "Maggie Walker." She was manufactured in sizes from 15in. (38.1cm) to 23in. (58.4cm). She is marked on the head "ALEXANDER."

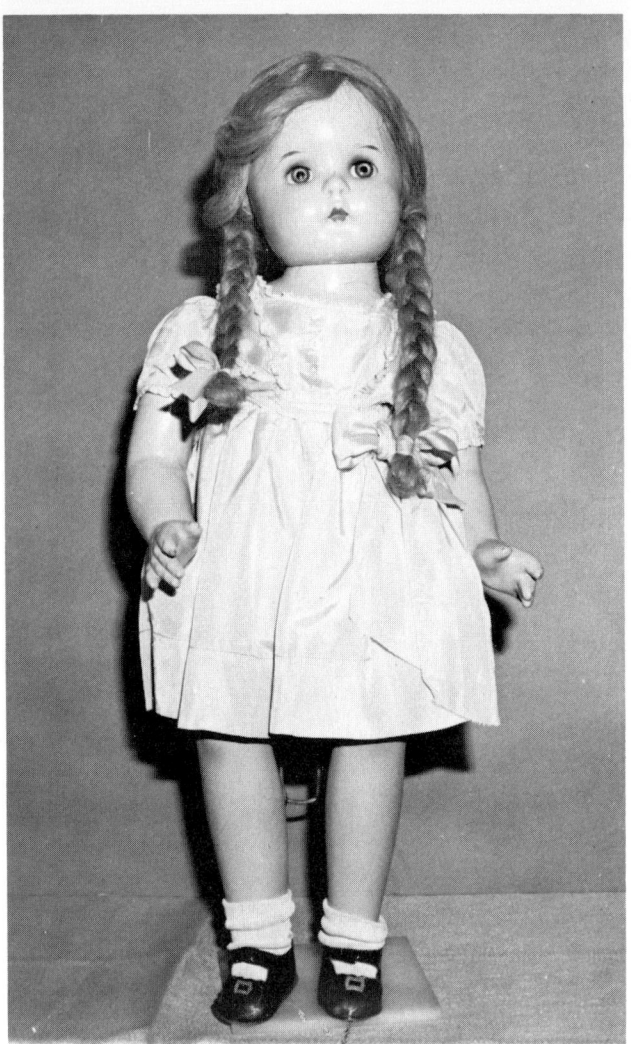

Related to the "Jeannie Walker" face is that of this doll also listed in the 1942-1943 catalog as a "Special Girl Doll." She is 22in. (55.9cm) tall with a composition head, shoulderplate, arms and legs; her torso is cloth and her hair is blonde and braided. Her dress is of pink taffeta. The clothing is labeled "Madame Alexander," but there are no marks on the doll. (*Vivian C. Flagg Collection.*)

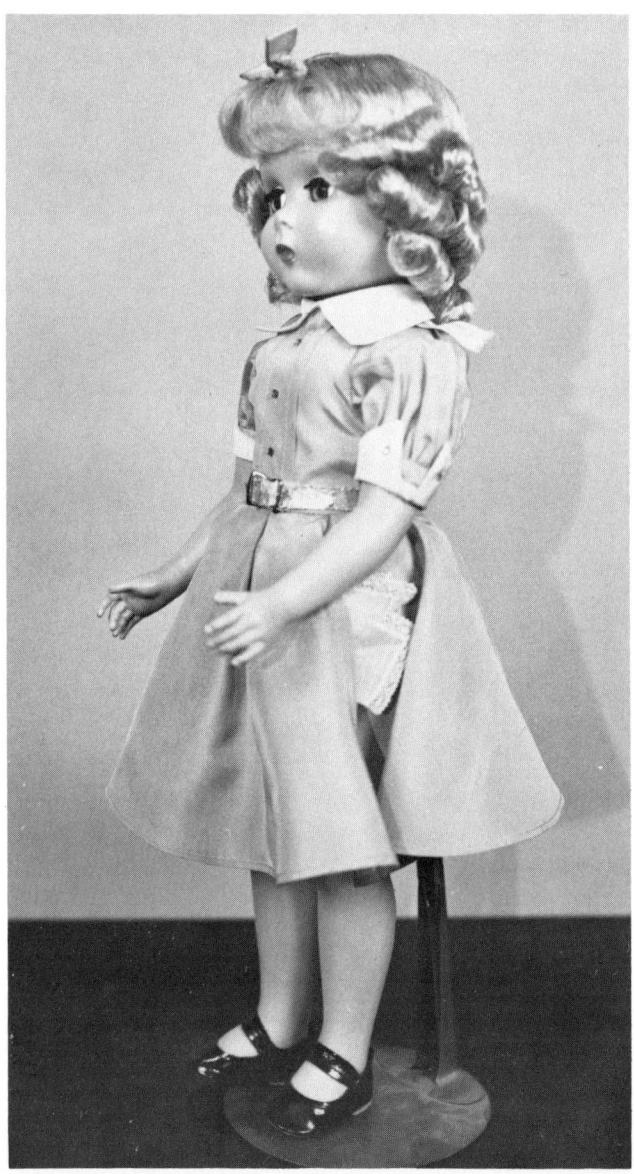

This "Maggie" is 17in. (43.2cm) tall. She has a lovely curly blonde wig. Madame Alexander was switching from mohair and human hair wigs to synthetics which could be combed, washed and curled. The dolls who had these washable wigs carried a small pink box which contained curlers and a comb. "Maggie" is wearing a pink taffeta shirtwaist dress with a flared skirt. Her collar and cuffs are in white. At her waist is a gold belt. In her pocket is a white cotton handkerchief. She is wearing hose and strap shoes, although most "Maggies" wore ankle socks. Her dress is tagged "Madame Alexander." (*Maxine Salaman Collection.*)

"Polly Pigtails" dates from 1949. She came in at least three sizes: 15in. (38.1cm), 18in. (45.7cm) and 20in. (50.8cm). This "Polly Pigtails" is wearing a below-the-knee plaid dress with a bias cut skirt bottom, puff sleeves and a white piqué collar and cuffs. Her straw hat has a wide brim. She has white knee socks and black strap shoes. Her dress is labeled "Polly Pigtails" and she has her cloverleaf wrist label. Her blonde pigtail wig is of nylon. Lorraine Burdick says that she was named for *Parents Magazine* pre-teen publication *Polly Pigtails*. (*Maxine Salaman Collection.*)

"Kathy" is probably from 1951 as she has her Fashion Academy Award tag. She is wearing roller skates and a sports outfit consisting of plaid pedal pushers, a white organdy blouse and a red corduroy weskit. She also has a watch fob! A black velvet cap with a red feather perches jauntily on her head. Her wig is shiny blonde with bangs and braids. She is 15in. (38.1cm) tall, but was also issued in 18in. (45.7cm) and 23in. (58.4cm) sizes. (*Maxine Salaman Collection.*)

"Alice in Wonderland" dates from 1950 and 1951. She was offered in 15in. (38.1cm), 18in. (45.7cm) and 23in. (58.4cm) sizes. This "Alice" has the traditional blonde wig pulled back on the side and held with a bow with shoulder-length curls in back. She is wearing a peach taffeta dress, but some came in blue dresses. Her white organdy pinafore is edged with lace and rickrack at the neckline. She has long white stockings and black shoes. She dates from 1951 as she is wearing her Fashion Academy Award necklace. Behind "Alice" is an advertising poster from the period featuring an "Alice in Wonderland" doll. This is another example of Madame Alexander reissuing a doll in a different form, having previously offered her in cloth and composition. See pages 7 and 33. (*Maxine Salaman Collection.*)

Left: "Annabelle" was made in 1952 only. Called Kate Smith's "Annabelle," she was dressed like the little girl in Kate Smith's book *Stories of Annabelle*. She came in 15in. (38.1cm), 18in. (45.7cm) and 23in. (58.4cm) sizes. "Annabelle" is wearing a pink pique princess style dress with a Peter Pan collar. This is topped by a turquoise cotton knit sweater with her name embroidered across the front. She has blonde hair with bangs, pulled back on the sides and held by a ribbon. This "Annabelle" is 20-1/2in. (52.1cm) tall; however this size is not listed in the catalog, which gives a 23in. (58.4 cm) size. I have noticed that these dolls with the "Maggie" faces often do not quite measure up to the 23in. (58.4cm) size as listed. In measuring dolls, one must allow even up to 2in. (5.1cm) in a larger doll for variation. (*Maxine Salaman Collection.*)

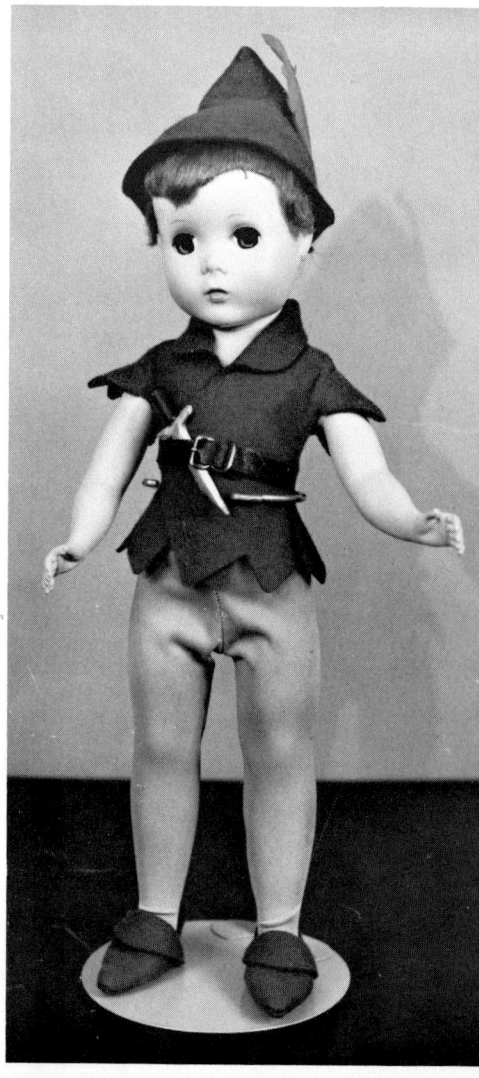

Center: "Nat," one of the dolls from Louisa May Alcott's *Little Men*, was issued in 1952 only. There were three boys in the set; the others were "Tommy Bangs" and "Stuffy." It is surprising that this charming set was made for one year only. If it were repeated today, it would certainly be an instant hit with collectors. The "Little Men" were made only in the 15in. (38.1cm) size, catalog #1501. "Nat" wears brown pants, a white shirt with a ribbon tie and a gold felt blazer with matching cap. Tan suede boots complete his costume. On his wrist is his Fashion Academy Award tag. Both his hair and eyes are dark. (*Maxine Salaman Collection.*)

Right: "Peter Pan" was made in 1953 only. He is dressed just like his namesake from the Walt Disney film who came to take Wendy away to Never-Never Land. His costume consists of a green felt pixie hat with a feather, a green felt jacket and shoes and brown nylon tights. "Peter Pan" came in the 15in. (38.1cm) size only, catalog #1505. He has auburn hair and brown eyes. (*Maxine Salaman Collection.*)

"Rosamund Bridesmaid" is a very striking doll with her softly curled auburn hair and large brown eyes. She was issued in 1953 only and came in both 15in. (38.1cm) and 18in. (45.7cm) sizes, catalog numbers #1551 and #1851. (The first two digits of the catalog numbers are usually the height in inches.) "Rosamund" is wearing a gown of pink taffeta with a nylon tulle overskirt, tulle ruffle on the bodice and tulle straps. Her matching half cap has flower trim on each side. She has a walking body. Her dress is labeled "Madame Alexander." (*Edna Black Collection.*)

Little Women

"Little Women" was one of the most lasting of the Alexander series, being produced almost continuously from 1933 until the present except for possibly a short time in the 1940s. The hard plastic version of the "Little Women" dolls was out in 1949 and possibly as early as 1948. They measure 14-15in. (35.6-38.1cm) in size, and were cataloged as #1500. There were a great variety of costumes on this hard plastic series which was in production until 1956. All of the costumes were beautifully designed in typical Alexander fashion with much attention to ruffles and trims. Apparently not all of the variations are pictured in the yearly catalogs and some outfits were changed during the year. There were also some variations in the dolls themselves. Some were light complexioned and some had the suntan look. In 1950 and 1951 they had larger hands with individual fingers; in other years the hands were small with fingers all together. In the mid-1950s they were made with bending knees. The first year or so the dolls' clothes were tagged only "Madame Alexander." Later they were given individual name labels. Usually "Beth" and "Jo" have the "Maggie" face and "Amy," "Meg" and "Marmee" have the "Margaret" face. The first set did not include a "Marmee" who was added probably in 1950 or 1951 as she is listed in the 1952 catalog. A May 1949 *Playthings* article mentions only the four girls and suggests a tie-in with the film *Little Women*, which had just been released, as a marvelous publicity item. This version included Margaret O'Brien as Beth, Elizabeth Taylor as Amy, Janet Leigh as Meg and June Allyson as Jo.

This set is like that shown in the 1952 Alexander catalog. They will be described from left to right.

"Amy," so tagged, has the most marvelous platinum floss wig with bangs and long looped curls. This is difficult to describe, so two close-up views of her are shown on page 45. Apparently not all "Amys" have this particularly fancy style, especially those from 1951 on, which have a wig styled more like "Meg's." Her dress is pink cotton with a print bodice.

"Meg," so tagged, has blonde hair with bangs pulled up from the sides to the top with a pageboy effect in the back. She is wearing a pink dress with a print apron.

"Jo," so tagged, wears a green rayon gaberdine dress with tatted trim on the bodice and sleeves. She has white organdy undersleeves. Her brown hair is pulled to the back.

"Beth," so tagged, is dressed in a charming blue and white checked cotton gown with a white organdy bodice. Her skirt has dark blue and red rickrack trim on the waistband and outlines an apron effect. Her brown hair is partially pulled to the top and gently curled across the bottom. (*All from Rosemary Dent Collection.*)

"Beth"

Front and back views of "Amy"

 Margaret Face

The "Margaret O'Brien" doll was carried over from the composition dolls and continued in hard plastic in 1948. For a complete discussion of this doll, see page 33. The "Margaret" mold with its sweet face continued to be a popular number and Madame Alexander used it for dozens of dolls beside "Margaret O'Brien" herself. It is usually marked "ALEXANDER" on the head.

The "Margaret O'Brien" pictured is 14in. (35.6cm) tall. She was made in hard plastic in 1948 only. She is wearing a blue wool jumper with braid trim over a white blouse. Her straw hat is red. She has her typical brown wig with looped braids. The wrist tag contains a later photo of the star and was added by the owner. Her dress is labeled "Margaret O'Brien." (*Maxine Salaman Collection.*)

The "Fairy Queen" was also a carry-over from composition. She is shown on page 34. This one is a 14in. (35.6cm) size wearing a white tulle overskirt, peplum and sleeves with rosebud decoration. She has gold braid on her bodice and tiara. She is carrying her magic wand and wearing her cloverleaf wrist tag. Her hair is auburn. Some of these dolls had wings, but this one does not. (*Maxine Salaman Collection.*)

Just a darling doll is this "McGuffey Ana" from 1948. She has such a wistful little face. For this doll, Madame Alexander dipped back to the popular composition doll with the "Princess Elizabeth" face shown on page 26. "McGuffey Ana" is wearing a white organdy dress topped by a pink corduroy coat with fur-trimmed collar and cuffs. She is carrying a matching muff. Her bonnet is of pink felt. Long white stockings and brown snap shoes complete her costume. Her blonde wig is in the traditional style with curly bangs and pigtails. She is also shown in a close-up version. (*Maxine Salaman Collection.*)

Above: This lovely 14in. (35.6cm) bride is probably from 1948 or 1949. Her hair is a beautiful shade of red with soft curls framing her face. Her stiff bride's cap has a corsage of flowers at each side. A veil of tulle edged with lace cascades down her back. Her gown is white organza over taffeta and she carries a tiny bouquet. She also has her green foil wrist tag. Her gown in tagged "Madame Alexander." (*Maxine Salaman Collection.*)

Top right: "Babs" the Skating Doll is from 1948 to 1950. She was manufactured in 15in. (38.1cm), 18in. (45.7cm) and 21in. (53.3cm) sizes in two versions, one with the "Maggie" face and one with the "Margaret" face. This 18in. (45.7cm) "Babs," so tagged, is wearing a beautiful costume of blue satin with blue maribou trim at the hem and sleeves. Her cap matches and has a flower corsage which is repeated on her ribbon sash. Her skates are gold. (*Maxine Salaman Collection.*)

Right: The date of manufacture of this 17in. (43.2cm) "Margaret Rose," so tagged, was between 1948 and 1953, probably closer to 1953, the date of her sister's coronation. "Margaret Rose" has lovely wavy blonde hair with bangs and soft curls. She is wearing a pastel gown of pink and blue with lace cap-like sleeves and a flower corsage on her shoulder and at her waist with a ribbon cascade. Her gathered overskirt also is topped by a peplum. This doll is known to have been made in a 14in. (35.6cm) size. She was also issued in 18in. (45.7cm) as one of the Beau Arts Creations in 1953 (#202B) for the coronation of Elizabeth II. (*Maxine Salaman Collection.*)

"Mary Martin," star of the popular *South Pacific*, was made in doll form in 1949 and 1950. The May 1950 *Playthings* ad showed her as "Knuckle-Head Nellie" in a white evening gown. In this version a 17in. (43.2cm) "Mary Martin" is wearing a white sailor suit with her name embroidered over the pocket. This suit is a copy of an original one. She has an interesting short caracul wig. This doll was also made in a 14in. (35.6cm) size. (*Maxine Salaman Collection.*)

Nearly every little girl dreams of one day being a lovely and graceful ballerina. Madame Alexander understands these fantasies and has nearly always had ballerinas in her line.

This "Nina Ballerina" was made from 1949-1951 in 15in. (38.1 cm), 17in. (43.2cm), 19in. (48.3cm) and 23in. (58.4 cm) sizes. She has lovely blonde hair with fluffy bangs in the front, the rest pulled to the back of her head and caught up with a garland of flowers. Her dress is white or silver taffeta with a tulle overskirt and sleeves. Silver rickrack sparkles as trim while rosebuds decorate shoulder and waist. She has her cloverleaf wrist tag as well as a clothing label marked "Nina Ballerina." She is also shown in a close-up version. (*Edna Black Collection.*)

Margaret Face continued on page 50

Left: 14in. (35.6cm) "Miss America"; all-original. (*Maxine Salaman Collection.*)

Middle: 16in. (40.6cm) Composition "Kate Greenaway"; all-original. (*Edna Black Collection.*)

Above: 18in. (45.7cm) Composition and cloth "Baby McGuffey" with flirty eyes. (*Barbara Crescenze Collection.*)

Above: 16in. (40.6cm) Cloth "Little Em'ly"; all-original. (*Marjorie Yocom Collection.*)

Right: 18in.(45.7cm)Composition "Hansel and Gretel"; all-original. (*Maxine Salaman Collection.*)

Margaret Face continued from page 48

"Cinderella" and "Prince Charming" are from probably 1950. They were made in the 14in. (35.6cm) size only. Both have their name wrist tags. "Cinderella" is wearing a pale blue satin gown with puffed panniers studded with rhinestones. Her blonde hair is pulled back from her face and crowned with a gold tiara. "Prince Charming" has a pastel brocade tunic, Juliet sleeves with gold braid and a stand-up collar also with gold braid. His tights are decorated with a gold garter and his cap and cape match his tunic. (*Maxine Salaman Collection.*)

One of the loveliest Alexander hard plastic dolls is this 21in. (53.3cm) "Piper Laurie" probably from 1950. Not only is the coloring of her face beautifully done, but she has the most gorgeous red hair, pulled to the back and caught up with a corsage of blue flowers. Her dress is organza over pink taffeta with silver braid and navy sequin trim. Her dress is tagged "Madame Alexander." Her wrist booklet was made by her owner. She is also shown in a close-up photograph. (*Maxine Salaman Collection.*)

Left: "Cynthia" was made in 1952 and 1953 in 15in. (38.1cm), 18in. (45.7cm) and 22in. (55.9 cm) sizes, catalog #1530, #1830 and #2330. This 22in. (55.9cm) "Cynthia," so tagged, is wearing a pink organdy dress with three rows of lace-edged ruffles around the skirt. Her yoke, sleeves and neckline are all lace-edged. She has black hair pulled back and tied with a ribbon and dark brown eyes. She also has a walking mechanism. (*Maxine Salaman Collection.*)

Right: This 17in. (43.2cm) doll is probably from 1950. Her dress is tagged only "Madame Alexander" and she has not been specifically identified. She is wearing a rose taffeta dress with flowers and black velvet trim. It is fully gathered around the hips. Her short full sleeves are edged with black lace and flowers, and her black straw hat is trimmed with the same flowers. (*Maxine Salaman Collection.*)

 *"Godey Lady" Dolls of 1950*

Godey's Lady's Book was the magazine published in Philadelphia that American ladies depended upon for most of the 19th century to guide them in the realm of fashion. Over 100,000 of them read it, not just as a fashion magazine, but as a general journal for women. It contained poetry, short stories, recipes, patterns; articles on crafts, sports considered appropriate for women, gardening, music and art; general advice, and other tidbits to enhance everyday life. It was read by the society matrons in New York and Boston, as well as the ladies in the small towns of the American West, whose copies took many months to arrive from Philadelphia.

It was to the pages of this magazine that Madame Alexander turned for fashionable frocks in which to dress her "Godey Lady" dolls of 1950.

This lady is wearing a gold taffeta frock. Her bodice is simple with only braid for decoration, repeated on the ends of the sleeves which also have white undersleeves. The skirt is full with a pleated ruffle around the hem. Her blonde hair is elaborately styled with coils at each ear and a garland across the crown of her head. (*Maxine Salaman Collection.*)

Godey Lady continued on page 54

Above left: 14in. (35.6cm) Hard plastic "Prince Charming" and "Cinderella"; all-original. (*Maxine Salaman Collection.*)

14in. (35.6cm) Composition "Wendy Ann"; all-original. (*Barbara Crescenze Collection.*)

12in. (30.5cm) Hard plastic "Cinderella" in ball gown with "Lissy" face; all-original. (*Maxine Salaman Collection*)

20in. (50.8cm) Composition "McGuffey Ana"; all-original. (*Rosemary Dent Collection.*)

14 in. (35.6cm) Hard plastic "Godey Bride"; all-original. (*Maxine Salaman Collection.*)

12in. (30.5cm) Hard plastic set of "Little Women" and "Laurie" with "Lissy" faces; all-original. (*Maxine Salaman Collection.*)

Left: 15in. (38.1cm) Composition "Alice in Wonderland"; all-original. (*Barbara Crescenze Collection.*)
Middle: 13in. (33cm) Composition "McGuffey Ana"; all-original. (*Barbara Crescenze Collection.*)
Right: 13in. (33cm) Composition "Jane Withers"; all-original. (*Rosemary Dent Collection.*)

Godey Lady continued from page 51

The frocks appear to have been based upon styles popular during the 1860s and 1870s in a somewhat simplified version, of course, as most of the styles of that period were very elaborate, even those used for everyday dresses.

All of the "Godey Lady" dolls are 14in. (35.6 cm) tall and of hard plastic with the green foil cloverleaf tags on their wrists. The ladies all have "Margaret" faces; their clothing carries the label "Godey Lady." The gentleman has a "Maggie" face; his clothing is labeled "Madame Alexander."

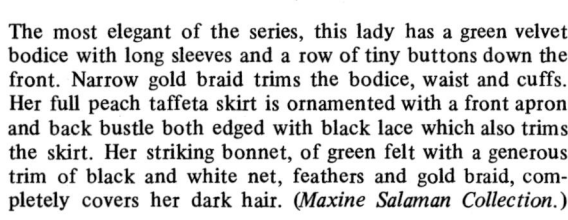

This pink taffeta frock has a full gored skirt topped by a basque with a white inset in the front and long side panels with glossy trim. The matching bonnet is trimmed with white tulle and feathers. The lady's lovely red hair with bangs in the front is caught up in a black snood at the back. (*Maxine Salaman Collection.*)

The most elegant of the series, this lady has a green velvet bodice with long sleeves and a row of tiny buttons down the front. Narrow gold braid trims the bodice, waist and cuffs. Her full peach taffeta skirt is ornamented with a front apron and back bustle both edged with black lace which also trims the skirt. Her striking bonnet, of green felt with a generous trim of black and white net, feathers and gold braid, completely covers her dark hair. (*Maxine Salaman Collection.*)

The lovely bride would be in style anywhere anytime. Her shining white satin gown has interest at the waist with lace-edged panniers and a back bustle with a full gathered train. Her veil cap frames her face and lace-edged tulle cascades down her back. She is carrying a traditional bride's bouquet. Her blonde hair is elaborately styled with curly bangs and sides pulled to the top and back with a mass of curls. (*Maxine Salaman Collection.*)

The gentleman is certainly reflective of the Victorian period. His trousers are lavender with a black stripe down the sides. His white satin shirt has lace ruffles down the front. His black gaberdine coat has a purple taffeta lining and is styled with tails. He wears a boutonniere in his lapel. His blonde hair is parted in the middle and is styled with the popular side curls and sideburns of the period. (*Maxine Salaman Collection.*)

12in. (30.5cm) Set of composition "Dionne Quintuplet Toddlers"; all-original. (*Virginia Ann Heyerdahl Collection.*)

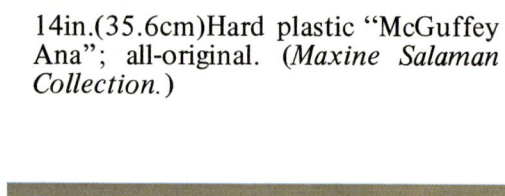

14in. (35.6cm) Hard plastic "McGuffey Ana"; all-original. (*Maxine Salaman Collection.*)

29in. (73.7cm) Vinyl and cloth "Alice in Wonderland." (*Edna Black Collection.*)

11in. (27.9cm) Hard Plastic "Godey Portrettes"; all-original. (*Maxine Salaman Collection.*)

Glamour Girls of 1953

A breath-taking series of seven ladies was created by Madame Alexander in 1953 only (at least they appear only in the catalog for that year). Both the "Maggie" and "Margaret" faces were used for these dolls, but the factory was not always consistent in confining one face to one particular doll. All of the "Glamour Girls" are 18in. (45.7cm) tall and made completely of hard plastic with a walking mechanism. All of them have "Madame Alexander" tags on their clothes and are carrying a marked Alexander hatbox containing curlers and a comb. All of the costumes are of the Civil War period Gone-with-the-Wind-type with full skirts, tiny waists and hoop skirts. The stock numbers are from the Alexander catalog.

Right: In the same basic style as #2001A (above right), this frock is made from a bright blue cotton print with pink and white flowers and green leaves. The sheer puff sleeves have lace trim. Her bonnet of stiff white lace ties under the chin with long streamers. Her sheer white gloves are missing. (#2001B, "Margaret" face.) (*Maxine Salaman Collection.*)

Below: This frock is made of a pink polished cotton print with green leaves. Black braid trim edges the top and bottom of the skirt ruffle. Black lace accents the sweetheart neckline and puff sleeves. She has a large green satin bow sash in the back. Her natural straw hat is trimmed with pink roses, black tulle and tie streamers. (#2001C, "Margaret" face.) (*Maxine Salaman Collection.*)

Above: This lady's frock has pink embossed flowers on a white polished cotton background. The low neck is accented with braid trim as is the lower skirt. Her black taffeta and lace bonnet ties under her chin. Black lace gloves complete her costume. (#2001A, "Margaret" face.) (*Maxine Salaman Collection.*)

Right: This frock has a very full bright red taffeta skirt and white taffeta sleeves and bodice. It is topped by a gray "fur" stole with a tiny red taffeta collar and black velvet ribbon tie. The matching bonnet is unadorned but styled with a circle brim and a gathered crown. (#2010A, "Maggie" face.) (*Maxine Salaman Collection.*)

This frock is of lustrous white taffeta accented by a wide red sash and tiny red rosebuds down the side of the skirt. Her sheer sleeves and scoop neckline are edged with white lace. A large picture hat of white horsehair with red rosebud trim frames her face. (#2010B, "Margaret" face.) (*Maxine Salaman Collection.*)

One of the most stunning gowns of the series is this one with a pale pink taffeta skirt and tiny puff sleeves. The bodice is of black velvet, and black velvet ribbon also trims the sleeves. The lady wears a corsage of pink and white flowers with black velvet streamers at her waist. Her black straw lace bonnet has pink rosebuds at the sides and large tulle ties. (#2010C, "Maggie" face.) (*Maxine Salaman Collection.*)

Having come to the throne of Great Britain in 1952, Queen Elizabeth II has been honored many times in a doll creation by Madame Alexander. The first after her coronation is this beautiful version wearing a gold and white taffeta brocade gown adorned with the jewel-studded blue sash of the Order of the Garter which crosses her left shoulder. Her pearl necklace, earrings, bracelet and jewel-studded gold coronet are all befitting a queen. She is also wearing the traditional long white gloves. (#2020A, "Margaret" face.) She is accompanied by Prince Philip also made in 1953, using the "Margaret" face but not listed in the catalog. (*Maxine Salaman Collection.*)

Winnie Face

A new child face appeared in the Alexander catalog in 1953. It was that of "Winsome Winnie Walker," and winsome is exactly the word to describe this face, which has a serious expression and a pretty shaped mouth with peaked upper lip. This face came on dolls 15in. (38.1cm), 18in. (45.7cm) and 25in. (63.5cm) tall. The 1953 "Winnie" was a hard plastic walker.

Also in 1954 the face was issued as "Sweet Violet," catalog #18788, in this outfit. She is unusual in that her body is entirely of hard plastic, but is ball-jointed like that of the old German dolls. Also, she is a walker. "Sweet Violet" is dressed appropriately for her name in a fitted lavender faille coat over a simple pink taffeta dress. Her flower-trimmed hat is of purple velvet with ties under the chin. A white fur muff and purple suede shoes complete her outfit. She is tagged "Madame Alexander." (*Maxine Salaman Collection.*)

Here she is in her catalog photo wearing a full organdy dress trimmed with lace, tucks and tiny pearl buttons. Her fancy bonnet frames her face. In her hatbox are curlers and a comb. (*Alexander Catalog Illustration.*)

In 1954, the "Winnie" face became "Winsome Binnie Walker" and she was offered as a hard plastic walking doll in the same sizes as "Winsome Winnie Walker."

Right: In 1955, the face was used for "Binnie Walker," and was offered in three different outfits in 15in. (38.1cm), 18in. (45.7cm) and 25in. (63.5cm) sizes. This year, in addition to walking, she had jointed knees and soft vinyl jointed arms. Here "Binnie" is wearing a checked taffeta dress trimmed with sparkling stones on the bodice and three rows of rickrack on the skirt. She has a hoop petticoat, a straw hat and a pigtail hairdo. Catalog numbers are #1511, #1811 and #2511. (*Edna Black Collection.*)

This "Mary Ellen" of 1954 and 1955 appears to be another use of the "Winnie" face in a much larger size, 31in. (78.7 cm). Her head and body are child proportioned; she also walks and turns her head; the 1955 version has soft jointed arms and jointed knees. "Mary Ellen" came in several fancy long gowns, as well as child outfits. Pictured here she is wearing a blue taffeta dress with three rows of lace trim at the neckline, puffed sleeves and a ribbon sash with rosette trim. This dress is not shown on her in the Alexander catalog, but the same style is shown on a small "Binnie." Apparently these dolls had dress styles in common. She is marked on the head ALEXANDER. Her clothing is tagged "Mary Ellen." (*Maxine Salaman Collection.*)

 Cissy Face

The "Cissy" fashion doll with a new face was introduced in 1955. She was all of hard plastic with legs jointed at the knee and soft arms jointed at the elbows. "Cissy" was advertised as "the doll with a figure and features of a debutante." The ad continues: "Her long slim body, her delicately molded bosom, and her beautifully shaped feet that wear only high heeled shoes made just for her and her elegant costumes designed for her alone make CISSY the shining wonder of the doll world." The first "Cissys" were also walkers. A complete line of clothing designed by Madame Alexander was available for her including lingerie, sportswear, street clothes, evening clothes and accessories. "Cissy" herself was made until 1959, but her face was used for portrait dolls until 1962. She is 20-21in. (50.8-53.3cm) tall.

Here is "Cissy" from 1956, catalog #2027. She is wearing a stunning traveling outfit of a black and white checked circle skirt with a red lining, a white piqué blouse and a black bolero jacket. Her white straw hat has a red rose. Other red accents are on her blouse, shoes and can-can petticoat. This "Cissy" is unusual because of her brown hair; most are blondes. Some "Cissys" carried hatboxes containing curlers and a comb. Her owner thought the black poodle added a chic touch. Her clothes are labeled "Cissy." Her head is marked ALEXANDER. (*Maxine Salaman Collection.*)

This "Cissy" as Queen is catalog #2281 from 1958. She is wearing a cream and gold brocade gown with a long back train, a square cut neckline and ruffle sleeves. Her gold tiara sparkles with gems as does her blue sash of the Order of the Garter. Earrings, long white gloves and a bracelet complete her outfit. (*Maxine Salaman Collection.*)

This "Cissy" is from 1957, catalog #2173. She wears a very formal black velvet gown with princess styling. On her white fur cape is a corsage of flowers. Diamond earrings and necklace complete her ensemble. Her blonde hair is elaborately arranged. She is also shown in a close-up view. (*Edna Black Collection.*)

Companies have sometimes used dolls in advertising their products. A very interesting series by Yardley produced in 1956 and 1957 featured Madame Alexander's "Cissy" doll. These ads appeared in *Ladies Home Journal* as well as *McCall's* and several Sunday newspaper magazine supplements.

This "Cissy" has shiny red hair and blue eyes. Her dress is white in a simple style with a scoop neck, raglan sleeves and a full skirt. She has a pearl necklace, but no earrings. (*Virginia Ann Heyerdahl Collection.*)

"Cissy" here is wearing a gray dress with a very full skirt. The bodice buttons down the front with tiny pearl buttons; it has a low vee neck and tiny cape sleeves. Her hair is blonde and her eyes are gray. A pearl necklace and earrings complete her ensemble. (*Virginia Ann Heyerdahl Collection.*)

Here "Cissy" wears a bright pink outfit. Her slim pink toreador pants are topped by a button-down front tunic with a scoop neck and cape sleeves. Her hair is auburn. She is wearing gold loop earrings, a bracelet and gold sandals. (*Virginia Ann Heyerdahl Collection.*)

This "Cissy" has bright blue eyes and a matching bow in her blonde hair. This doll has more vivid coloring than those in the other ads. (*Virginia Ann Heyerdahl.*)

Here is "Cissy" wearing an olive green outfit which appears to be a sheath dress topped by s short jacket banded in gold ribbon. Her hair is strawberry blonde again and her eyes are hazel. Her jewelry consists of a gold link necklace, round earrings and a bangle bracelet. (*Virginia Ann Heyerdahl Collection.*)

Another "Cissy" with red hair, this one is wearing a white gown with a high waist, a square neckline with pink inset in bodice and puff sleeves in a pink rosebud print. (*Virginia Ann Heyerdahl Collection.*)

This blonde-haired "Cissy" wears a rose gown in a very formal style with a low neckline, short sleeves and a stole effect around her shoulders fastened with a large pink rose. (*Virginia Ann Heyerdahl Collection.*)

Two other ads have been reported: one in which she is wearing a gray dress and holding a bar of soap; the other wearing a lavender and white shirtwaist dress, the ad featuring a bottle of English Lavender.

Elise Face

Advertised in 1957 as a brand new doll "from the tips of her toes to the crown of her head," "Elise" was 16-1/2in. (41.9cm) tall, later stretched to 17in. (43.2cm) and 18in. (45.7cm). She was made until 1964 in this hard plastic version. "Elise" had vinyl arms jointed at the elbows, and hard legs jointed at the knees and ankles so that she could wear high or low heels. "Elise" could be purchased dressed in street clothes, or in special bride, formal or ballerina outfits. For the first two years of issue, she could also be purchased as a basic doll in underwear only with a large variety of separate dresses, coats, hats and accessories available. She was marked on the head:
"ALEXANDER"
On the body she was marked:
MME
ALEXANDER

Above: This "Elise," a ballerina of 1957, catalog #1635, is wearing a tutu of white tulle with a satin bodice. A garland of pink and white flowers decorates her dress, and a crown of the same flowers tops her blonde hair. *(Maxine Salaman Collection.)*

Left: Truly regal is this "Elise" attired as Queen Elizabeth II of England. Her dress of satin brocade is decorated with the gem studded sash of the Order of the Bath. Her queenly jewels include pendant earrings and necklace, two bracelets and a ring. She is wearing long white gloves. Under her dress is a red net petticoat! Her hair is dark as is the Queen's. She is from 1963, catalog #1780. Also in this special portrait series were "Elise" as a Renoir lady in mauve taffeta and "Elise" as Scarlett O'Hara. *(Maxine Salaman Collection.)*

"Elise" of 1958, catalog #1736, is wearing a gorgeous garden party frock of sheer nylon sprinkled with flocked flowers and decorated with a corsage of sweetheart roses at her waist. Her horsehair picture hat is trimmed with flowers and net. "Elise" is wearing a pearl necklace and a "diamond" ring. The dark-haired version is more unusual as most seem to have blonde hair. Her dress is tagged "Elise." In 1966 "Elise" was issued in a new version with a vinyl head. *(Edna Black Collection.)*

Individual Faces

This 12in. (30.5cm) "Little Genius" is from 1949. She has a hard plastic head, arms and lower legs. Her body is of pink cloth and contains a cry box. Her blonde mohair wig is curly with two bows in the front. Her white organdy dress has pink ribbon trim and is tagged "Little Genius." Her eyes are blue, and she is marked ALEXANDER on her head. (*Joanna Ott Collection.*)

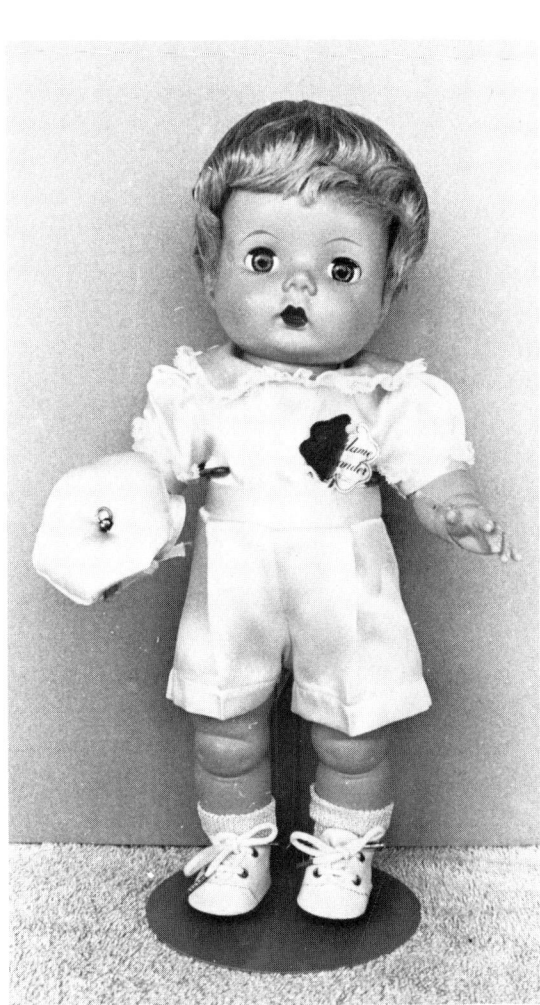

Here are two variations of a very unusual 12in. (30.5cm) hard plastic toddler marked ALEXANDER on his head. The first one has a blonde wig over his molded hair, sleep eyes and a closed rosebud mouth. His arms and legs are chubby with fat rolls at his knees. He is wearing a white satin outfit with lace trim on his shirt. On the pillow he carries the wedding ring. He is wearing his cloverleaf tag and is probably from the 1948-1950 period. Such a little charmer as a "Ringbearer"! (*Rhoda Shoemaker Collection; photograph courtesy of Rhoda Shoemaker.*)

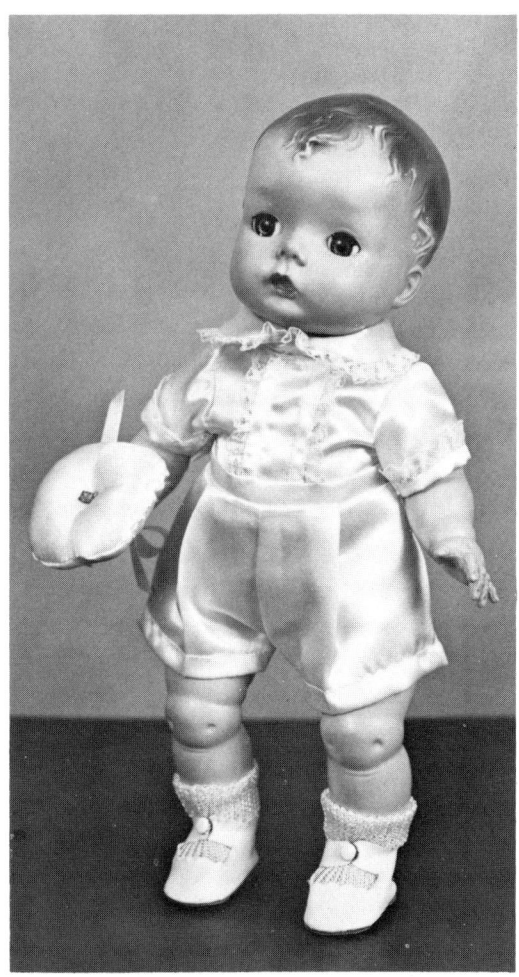

This version is the same size, but has the molded hair. His suit is a copy of the original. (*Maxine Salaman Collection.*)

One of the most beautiful dolls of her period is this 16-1/2in. (41.9cm) "Sleeping Beauty" of 1959, catalog #1895. She has the "Elise" body with jointed ankle and vinyl jointed arms. She also came in a 21in. (53.3cm) size using the "Cissy" body. Her gown is of light blue taffeta fading to lavender. Her gold crown is studded with rhinestones and her shimmering golden cape is of net brocade. She certainly has a regal and queenly bearing. Her original wrist tag reads: "Madame Alexander Presents Walt Disney's Authentic Sleeping Beauty." Her hair is blonde and her eyes are blue. (*Maxine Salaman Collection.*)

"Shari Lewis," of 1959 only, is a portrait doll of the television personality who, with her puppets, entertained on children's programs. She is all of hard plastic with a slim fashion-type body, and was made in two sizes, 14in. (35.6cm) and 21in. (53.3cm). The larger size used the "Cissy" body. "Shari" came in several different outfits. Here she is wearing an evening dress of yellow nylon taffeta with a bouffant overskirt of gold and yellow lace. Her bodice is simple with braid trim down the front, and around her long sleeves. Her taffeta sash has a corsage of roses. "Shari's" outfit is accented with necklace, earrings and bracelet. She has auburn hair and brown eyes. Her wrist tag shows "Shari" with one of her puppets, probably "Lamb Chop." She is marked "ALEXANDER" on her head; her dress is tagged "Shari Lewis." (*Maxine Salaman Collection.*)

Alexander-Kins

The "Alexander-Kins," introduced in 1953, have been one of the most enduring series created by Madame Alexander, and a good variety of them are still in production today; though the term *Alexander-Kins* is no longer used by the company, all of the 8in. (20.3cm) hard plastic dolls will be grouped in this category for convenience.

Little dolls have always been extremely popular with little girls. They are easy to carry and cuddle; just about anywhere a little girl goes, the doll can go too. Apparently these little Alexanders caught on right away for in the 1956 Alexander-Kins catalog, there are 73 different outfits in which one could purchase "Wendy." Or she could be purchased undressed and outfits could be chosen from among the wide variety of clothes and accessories offered for her.

This little 8in. (20.3cm) darling came all in hard plastic as do the current small dolls. Her face is sweet with a round look, chubby cheeks, tiny mouth and sleeping eyes with molded upper lashes and painted lower ones. Her wig was of a variety of colors and styles, most common of which was a cute little blonde girl style with a part in the middle, curly bangs and hair smooth to the neckline then curled gently. Following is a chart of production changes to help date these little ones.

1953—	7-1/2in. (19.1cm) straight legs, non-walkers, some with molded hair.
1954—	7-1/2in. (19.1cm) straight legs, walkers
1955—	8in. (20.3cm) straight legs, walkers
1956-1964—	8in. (20.3cm) bending knees, walkers
1965-1972—	8in. (20.3cm) bending knees, non-walkers
1973-present—	8in. (20.3cm) straight legs, non-walkers

Of course, there will be some overlapping during the years when body styles were being changed as current stock was being used up before the new models were used. There were also some changes in the plastic formula or finish over the years as well as subtle facial changes as molds were renewed. The early and walking dolls have a shiny finish and paler face color, due in part to fading. The later non-walking dolls have a matte finish with pinker tint. All are marked ALEX on the back of their torsos. Seeing a group of these charming little ones, it is not hard to understand how one could become attached to them.

"Wendy," also called "Wendy Ann" and "Wendykin" was produced from 1953 until 1965 in the little girl and special outfits.

In addition to her stylish little girl outfits to cover every possible activity or social event, "Wendy" was available in special outfits, such as "Little Women," storybook characters, period costumes and wedding clothes. And even as a boy doll called "Bill" or "Billy"!

The International series in beautifully designed provincial costumes from around the world was introduced in 1961. In 1965 Madame Alexander was honored by United States Ambassador to the United Nations, The Honorable Arthur Goldberg, on United Nations Day for her International dolls. This series is still in production although there have been additions and deletions over the years. With 37 countries now in production, it is the largest current series. In the late 1930s Madame Alexander also produced a wide variety of International dolls in composition.

"Storyland" category was added as an official title in 1965, although "Wendy" had previously been available in some of these outfits. There are currently 11 dolls in this series.

This 7-1/2in. (19.1cm) Alexander-Kin from 1953 is unusual in that he has molded hair. His blue suit is untagged, but is like that worn by Prince Charles (#397) of 1957, including the cap which was removed to show his molded hair. The photos of the dolls in the 1953 catalog are so tiny that it is difficult to identify anyone even with a magnifying glass, but several of the dolls do appear to have molded hair. Also, since this doll is a non-walker it appears to be of this date. (*Maxine Salaman Collection.*)

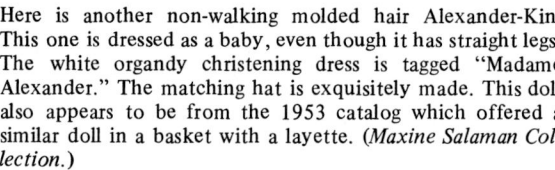

Here is another non-walking molded hair Alexander-Kin. This one is dressed as a baby, even though it has straight legs. The white organdy christening dress is tagged "Madame Alexander." The matching hat is exquisitely made. This doll also appears to be from the 1953 catalog which offered a similar doll in a basket with a layette. (*Maxine Salaman Collection.*)

This is a 7-1/2in. (19.1cm) "Victoria," catalog #0030C, from the "Me and My Shadow Series" of 1954. She was the matching miniature to an 18in. (45.7cm) Portrait doll. "Victoria" is wearing a slate blue taffeta full skirt and top draped in front and pulled to a bustle in the back. Narrow white braid, flowers and pearls trim her top. The tiny hat is of starched white lace with flower trim. She still has her fuchsia velvet reticule. Her dress is tagged "Alexander-Kins." (*H & J Foulke.*)

Dated 1954-1955 because she is a walker with straight legs, this "Wendy" has a tagged "Alexander-Kins" dress which does not seem to be shown in the catalog pictures. It is a darling dress of blue and white check with a full skirt and lace-edged puff sleeves. The white yoke has rickrack and lace trim as well as tiny buttons. Her hat is of white straw with a flower ornament. (*Edna Black Collection.*)

"Southern Belle," an Alexander favorite, is given yet another treatment in this 1956 bending-knee walker, which is 8in. (20.3cm) tall. Her pink taffeta gown has long sleeves, a bustle and a train in the back. The bodice is draped over a very full skirt. She is carrying a pink reticule, but is missing her straw hat. Her dress is tagged "Alexander-Kins." (*H & J Foulke.*)

On the right is the basic "Wendy" in the bending-knee version produced from 1956 until 1964, catalog #600. She is wearing pink and white checked panties and shoes and socks just like new. Sitting is 8in. (20.3cm) "Little Genius" made from 1956 until 1962. Her face is very similar to "Wendy's," but has an opening in her mouth for taking a bottle. She has a blonde fur wig. Her head is of hard plastic and her body is vinyl. She wears a pink and white checked dress with lace all around the yoke; the gathered skirt is edged with a ruffle at the hem. The lace on her matching bonnet frames her face. "Little Genius" was also available as a basic doll with panties, bonnet and booties. An extensive wardrobe was offered and could be purchased separately. All of her outfits were lovely and made with the great attention to detail which has always characterized Madame Alexander dolls. Her dress is tagged "Little Genius." (*Barbara Crescenze Collection.*)

This little "Wendy" is called "First Communion." She is an 8in. (20.3cm) bending-knee walker from 1957, catalog #395. This is a very hard-to-find outfit. Of course, she is dressed all in white including her flower headpiece, net veil, shoes and socks. Her dress is tagged "Alexander-Kins." Her pretty blonde hair is styled in braids. (*Joanna Ott Collection.*)

This close-up view shows the adorable new face of the 8in. (20.3cm) "Maggie Mixup" produced in 1960 and 1961. This doll is shown full length with her larger companion on page 87. "Maggie Mixup" is a darling imp with freckles, green eyes, straight red hair with bangs and, of course, her watermelon mouth which is so appealing. Her dress is an aqua check with a white collar and she wears a golden heart necklace. Her roller brim hat is of natural straw, and she wears black shoes and stockings. Some of these little dolls had blue eyes and/or a rosebud mouth, but all had red hair and freckles. The "Maggie Mixup" face was also used on some of the international dolls. (*Maxine Salaman Collection.*)

This set of Alexander-Kins as "Little Women" dates 1963 or 1964. "Laurie" was added to the group in 1966. They are all 8in. (20.3cm) tall and are bending-knee walkers except "Laurie," who has bending knees but does not walk. Starting on the left of the back row is "Amy" wearing a powder blue dress with a white organdy apron. She has a particularly fancy hairdo, as generally her hair is not fluffed out so much. "Laurie" has his typical navy blue and white outfit with matching cap. "Marmee" is wearing her maroon dress with an eyelet apron and dust cap. In the front row, "Jo" wears a blue print dress with an organdy blouse and a red apron. "Meg's" dress is lavender and white striped with an organdy pinafore. "Beth's" frock is a checked cotton with an eyelet pinafore. All are tagged with their own names. (*Jackie Dent Collection.*)

The "American Girl" from 1963 is catalog #388. She is very similar to "McGuffey Ana," as she is wearing a red print dress with a white eyelet apron. Her blonde pigtails are topped with a tiny straw hat having flower trim. She is 8in. (20.3cm) tall and a bending-knee walker. (*Edna Black Collection.*)

The "Amish Boy" and "Amish Girl," catalog #726 and #727, were made from 1966 until 1969. They are dressed in the somber colors of the "plain people" of the Lancaster, Pennsylvania region. (*Maxine Salaman Collection.*)

Left:
The 8in. (20.3cm) "Snow White" was made from about 1972 until 1977 exclusively for Disneyland and Disney World. Most will have straight non-walking legs as this doll and the "Alice in Wonderland" which follows was introduced during the transition period from bending knees to straight legs. "Snow White" is wearing the Disney colors: a gold taffeta skirt, a bodice of dark blue velvet with braid on the sleeves and a fuchsia taffeta cape edged with gold braid and a white stand-up collar. She has brown hair with a fuchsia hair band. Nylon pantyhose and black slippers are her footwear. Madame Alexander also made this doll in a 14in. (35.6 cm) size exclusively for Disney. (*Virginia Ann Heyerdahl Collection.*)

Right:
This 8in. (20.3cm) "Alice in Wonderland" also was made from about 1972 until 1977 exclusively for Disneyland and Disney World. She is wearing her traditional costume consisting of a blue cotton dress with a white collar and white lace and braid on the sleeves; her white cotton pinafore has a sash in the back. Her blonde hair is held back with a blue band. Several other small "Alice" dolls were made in 1955 and 1956. Both had blue taffeta dresses. The 1956 model (#590) had a crisp white pinafore; the 1955 design (#465) had a white eyelet pinafore. The 14in. (35.6cm) "Alice in Wonderland" in a similar costume was not exclusively for Disney and has been in the regular Alexander line since 1966. (*Virginia Ann Heyerdahl Collection.*)

 Lissy Face

"Lissy" was a new face in the Alexander catalog of 1956. Just 11-1/2in. (29.2cm) tall, her dainty and pert demeanor is very appealing to collectors. She was available in a series of street clothes and as a bride, bridesmaid or ballerina. A special ensemble included the doll and a nine-piece trousseau. In 1957 and 1958 she was also offered as a basic doll with a large variety of separate clothes and accessories. She is all of hard plastic with joints at the elbows and knees. Her clothes were labeled "Lissy," but the doll itself is unmarked.

In 1959 the "Lissy" face was used for the "Kelly" doll in the 12in. (30.5cm) size. She is listed in the catalog, but not pictured so many collectors are unaware of her. She was jointed at the shoulders and hips only, unlike "Lissy" who had elbow and knee joints as well.

This "Kelly" is wearing a blue and white checked cotton dress with a fuchsia pinafore trimmed with white rickrack. She hides a posy in her pocket. Her hair is blonde, and she wears tiny earrings. Her dress is tagged "Kelly." For the larger version of this doll see page 86. (Catalog #1102.) (*Edna Black Collection.*)

Here "Kelly" wears a party dress of pink nylon organdy. Her pleated skirt, sleeves and Peter Pan collar are all lace-edged. Her sash has a flower corsage at the side and some flowers ornament her pink straw hat. She also has tiny earrings. Her dress is tagged "Kelly." (Catalog #1110.) (*Maxine Salaman Collection.*)

"Katie" and "Tommy" were made by Madame Alexander in 1962 especially for the 100th Anniversary of F.A.O. Schwarz and were an exclusive item for them, so they are very difficult for collectors to find. "Katie" wears a yellow taffeta dress with tiny lace trimming and a wide reddish-brown velvet ribbon sash. Her white organdy dust cap has a matching ribbon. "Tommy" wears a blue turn-of-the-century suit with tiny buttons and a round collar. His straw hat has a rolled brim. Both of the dolls are tagged "Madame Alexander" and have their original wrist booklets. (*Maxine Salaman Collection.*)

In 1962 and 1963 the "Lissy" face was used for "Pamela" who was advertised as new and exciting. The feature which prompted these adjectives was that she had three interchangeable wigs which were held on by an adhesive strip on her head. She came in trousseau sets only. (Catalog #1280.) (*Maxine Salaman Collection.*)

In 1963 Madame Alexander issued the Classics Group of dolls which had the "Lissy" face and were 12in. (30.5cm). This "Southern Belle," catalog #1255, is wearing a lovely light blue taffeta dress with white lace trim and pink ribbon insertion at cuffs, square neckline and hem. Three rows of lace trim the cotton pantaloons which peek out from under her skirt. Her white straw bonnet has pink and white feathers and rosebuds and her sash matches her hat ribbons. The blonde wig is styled with long curls. Her dress is tagged "Madame Alexander." (*Maxine Salaman Collection.*)

Another of the Classics Group is this "McGuffey Ana," catalog #1258. Again Madame Alexander turns to McGuffey's Reader for a charming little girl. She wears a red velvet suit with a circle skirt and a short jacket with a white "fur" collar. The hat and mittens match. Traditional long white stockings and two-toned high-buttoned shoes complete her ensemble. She has "McGuffey Ana's" traditional blonde pigtails. Her dress is tagged "Madame Alexander." The third doll in the Classics Group was "Scarlett O'Hara" who is presented on page 93. (*Maxine Salaman Collection.*)

Not appearing in the catalogs, but shown in a booklet which accompanied the dolls is this unusual set of *Sound of Music* doll children all dressed in matching sailor-type outfits. Possibly these did not sell well as all were dressed alike and purchasers did not tend to buy several. For whatever reason, they were made for only a short time, so this 12in. (30.5cm) "Brigitta" with the "Lissy" face is a very difficult-to-find doll. She was made in about 1964 and is tagged "Brigitta." (*Maxine Salaman Collection.*)

The "Cinderella" with the "Lissy" face was a special doll for 1966 and was 12in. (30.5cm) tall. She was issued in two versions, #1230 "Before the Ball" and #1235 "Ball Gown." She was also available as a boxed set #1240 which included the doll in a ball gown with an extra scullery maid outfit. Certainly a most beautiful design is this ball gown of pale blue satin with wide blue lace trim at the neckline, sleeves and edge of the overskirt. A panel down the front of her dress is edged with sequins and nipped-in at the waist with rosebuds. A small tiara tops her fancy blonde hairdo. Her scullery outfit is a moss green dress and kerchief, an orange patched apron and a small broom. Her clothing is tagged "Cinderella." (*Maxine Salaman Collection.*)

The "Little Women" dolls were made with the "Lissy" face from 1957 until 1967 and were all 12in. (30.5cm) tall. The first years, the dolls were jointed at elbows and knees, but this feature was discontinued. "Laurie" was added to the series in 1967. The costumes changed almost every year. They are always colorful, attractive and eye-catching.

"Laurie" wears a navy blue double-breasted coat and matching cap, striped trousers and tie. "Jo" wears a red cotton jumper with white rickrack. Her white organdy blouse has tiny red buttons on the cuffs. (*Maxine Salaman Collection.*)

"Meg" on the left wears a pink cotton dress under a blue and white striped apron with rickrack trim. "Marmee" on the right has a gown of green taffeta with a white organdy bertha and a yellow taffeta apron. (*Maxine Salaman Collection.*)

"Beth" on the left wears a frock of turquoise polka dotted cotton with white organdy sleeves edged with turquoise rickrack. "Amy" on the right, wears a frock of blue cotton print with tiny yellow flowers and a daffodil yellow apron edged with rickrack trim. (*Maxine Salaman Collection.*)

"Laurie" dates from 1967 while all of the girls and "Marmee" are from 1959.

Cissette Face

A new doll introduced in 1957, "Cissette," just 10in. (25.4cm) tall, was a miniature fashion lady with a shaped bosom, a slim waist and long, slender arms and legs, all of hard plastic. She was jointed above the knee and had feet shaped for high heels. The basic "Cissette" did not have eye makeup. She was such an important item in the Alexander line that she had a small catalog all to herself. She was offered in dozens of outfits and came with dozens more of accessories. All of her dresses and gowns and sports clothes were designed in the latest fashion of the 1957-1963 years during which she was produced. Many of the "Cissette" dolls were unmarked although her clothes are labeled either "Cissette" or "Madame Alexander." Mark on torso (sometimes unmarked): MME
ALEXANDER

Clothing label: "Cissette"
MADAME ALEXANDER
NEW YORK, U.S.A.
or
Madame Alexander
New York
All Rights Reserved

Since "Cissette" herself is a fairly easy doll to find, this section will concentrate on the many special versions using the basic "Cissette" doll under a variety of different names which were produced until 1973.

Made in 1961 only, "Margot" is an elegant doll with a special hairdo pulled to the crown in a large chignon with two side curls on her left forehead. Her eyes are glamorized with a wide line stroke at each outer corner, three lighter strokes inside and eye shadow on the upper lid. She wore earrings and a tiny glued-on ring. Her clothing is labeled "Margot." She is a very difficult doll to find.

In this photo "Margot" is wearing a fashionable sheath dress for afternoon wear of lavender satin with a side drape held by a brooch. Her neckline is ornamented by a row of pearls, and her black velvet stole is trimmed with shiny beads. Rhinestone pendant earrings and black sandals complete her ensemble. (Catalog #910.) (*Maxine Salaman Collection.*)

"Cissette" here wears one of her ballerina costumes with a pink skirt of pleated tulle dotted with sequins, and a satin bodice with a tulle ruffle and tiny rosebuds at the shoulders. In her black hair is a crown of flowers. (Catalog #813, 1960.) (*Edna Black Collection.*)

This blue satin sheath gown is styled simply. The matching full-length stole has sequin and fringe trim. (Catalog #886.) (*Virginia M. Slade Collection.*)

This "Jacqueline" is wearing a pale pink satin gown with a bouffant skirt which has an inverted front pleat and a bow ornament. Her plain bodice has a square cut neckline. She is carrying a white beaded purse and is wearing a necklace, earrings and a hair ornament to complete her ensemble. She is also shown in a close-up view. (Catalog #885.) (*Virginia M. Slade Collection.*)

"Jacqueline" (Kennedy) was named after the young and fashionable first lady whose husband was elected President of the United States in 1960 although the Kennedy name was not used in the Alexander catalog. The nation was enthralled with the glamour of this attractive young family which brought an aura of youth and vitality into the White House. The social pages of the newspaper were filled with photos of her in stunning outfits. For the "Jacqueline" doll Madame Alexander used the basic "Cissette" doll with a special dark wig styled with a side part, a forehead curl and a row of soft curls around the hairline. She had the glamorized eyes with heavy lashes at the eye corners and three lighter strokes above. All of the dolls had earrings and a tiny glued-on ring. Apparently because of White House objections, "Jacqueline" was made in 1962 only. Her clothing was labeled "Madame Alexander," and the doll's wrist tag carried her name "Jacqueline."

In 1961 and 1962 a beautiful 21in. (53.3cm) version of "Jacqueline" was offered.

Here "Jacqueline" wears a sports outfit of turquoise pants and a jersey shirt. Her white "leather" jacket is accented with top-stitching. (Catalog #865.) (*Virginia M. Slade Collection.*)

Three Special Cissettes

Right:
Styled after the famous turn-of-the-century drawings by Charles Dana Gibson, this special edition "Cissette" has a gold wrist tag proclaiming her "Gibson Girl." Her black velvet skirt flares out from her tiny waist which is cinched by a fancy buckled belt. Her white organdy blouse has front buttons, puff sleeves, a lace front and a double row of lace on the sleeves. Her large straw hat is trimmed with flowers. This doll has a regular "Cissette" face without the eye shadow or special lashes. Her clothing is labeled "Cissette." (Catalog #760, 1963 only.) (*Maxine Salaman Collection.*)

Above: Show girl of the period of the Alaskan gold rush boom, "Klondike" also has a gold wrist tag. She wears a slim red gown of velvet trimmed with red braid and tulle ruffled sleeves. She also has a wide tulle ruffle at her hemline. Her fancy dark hairdo, in the same style as Margot's, is adorned with red feathers and a jeweled ornament. A double row of pearls, earrings and a bracelet complete her costume. Her dress is labeled "Madame Alexander." She was probably made in 1963 but is not shown in the catalogs. (*Maxine Salaman Collection.*)

Left:
Dressed in the style of the 1849 California gold rush, this doll is identified by her gold wrist tag as "Gold Rush." She is wearing an orange taffeta dress. Her full skirt has a front draped overskirt pulled into a back bustle with black lace trim. Tiny black buttons adorn her bodice and sleeves. The black hat trimmed with tulle and feathers slants fetchingly over her forehead covering her "Margot"-styled blonde hair. Her clothing is labeled "Madame Alexander." She was probably made in 1963, but is not shown in the catalogs. (*Maxine Salaman Collection.*)

Portrettes

Maxine Salaman calls the Portrettes "miniature pieces of perfection" and a look at these dolls proves her right. This series was made from 1968 through 1973 but the models differed from year to year. They are usually listed as 11in. (27.9cm). The "Cissette" doll was brought back into use with a great variety of hair styles and colors. The eyes were glamorized with shadow on the lids and accented with a heavy eyeline and three lighter ones at the outer corner of the eyes. On the left hand is a tiny glued-on ring. Looking at just a few of these elegant miniature confections is sufficient to understand why they are prizes so eagerly sought after by collectors.

"Southern Belle" is wearing a very full dress of stiff sheer white nylon. Her tiered skirt is trimmed with olive green ribbon under lace insertion and edged with lace ruffles. Her bodice with plunging neckline and three-quarter length sleeves has the same trim. She has blonde hair which is topped by a white nylon organdy hat trimmed with red roses and she carries a posy in her hand. Her dress is tagged "Southern Belle." (Catalog #1170, 1968.) (*The Doll Royalle.*)

"Melinda" is wearing a bright turquoise taffeta dress with a very full gathered skirt edged with a pleated ruffle and white loop braid; the white yoke and sleeves are both edged with lace ruffles and loop braid. Her blonde hair is covered by a white straw hat with aqua tulle ties and flower trim on the crown. Her clothing is labeled "Melinda." (Catalog #1173, 1968 only.) (*Maxine Salaman Collection.*)

The "Renoir" lady is very elegantly dressed in a navy blue taffeta gown with a pleated ruffle in front coming up to the waist in the back. Her collar is another pleated ruffle, and she wears a pink rosebud at her neckline. Her sleeves are trimmed with white lace. Her large red taffeta hat with a red rose really sets off the outfit. (Catalog #1175, 1968.) (*Maxine Salaman Collection.*)

Left: "Agatha" wears a dress of red velvet with princess style lines. Ecru lace trims her neckline and sleeves. A tiny brooch shines at her neckline. Topping her black hair is a red velvet hat covered with a fluff of red tulle. Her clothing is labeled "Agatha." (Catalog #1171, 1968 only.) (*Maxine Salaman Collection.*)

Right: "Godey" lady wears an elegant period gown of ecru lace over yellow taffeta. Two rows of yellow taffeta ruffles circle the skirt and one draws up into the back. Tiny yellow satin ribbons are sprinkled down the dress front. Ecru lace trims the neckline and sleeves. Her natural straw hat with rolled brim, trimmed with yellow net and white flowers, tops her beautiful auburn hair. Her clothes are labeled "Godey." (Catalog #1172, 1969.) The 1968 "Godey" has a similar dress of pink taffeta and ecru lace and a straw picture-style hat. (*Maxine Salaman Collection.*)

Jenny Lind the Swedish nightingale who was born in 1820 was made into a doll by Madame Alexander to honor the singer's 150th birthday. She was so overwhelmingly popular that crowds mobbed her wherever she went all around the whole world in the 1850s. Frances Cavanah wrote about her in two books for children *Jenny Lind and Her Listening Cat* and *Jenny Lind's America*. The "Jenny Lind" doll was on display in January 1970 at the Metropolitan Opera House in New York for a revival of an opera sung there many years ago by Jenny Lind herself.

"Jenny Lind" appears here in a pink satin concert dress with a very full skirt and a puffed overskirt. The scoop neckline and sleeves are edged with white lace. Her blonde hair is in period style, close to her head with poufs at her ears and curls close to the neck. Pink flowers adorn each side of her hair and also her bodice front. She is carrying a nosegay of flowers probably given to her by an admirer. Her dress is labeled "Jenny Lind." (Catalog #1171, 1969.) (*Maxine Salaman Collection.*)

Her 1970 outfit, catalog #1184, is similar to this one except for a higher neckline and the effect of an overskirt achieved with a curved lace outline and silk multi-color flower trim. The flowers at her neckline are also different.

"Jenny Lind" as she is pictured here also appeared in the 21in. (53.3cm) Portrait in 1969 and 1970, and in the 14in. (35.6cm) Mary Ann face version in 1970. From 1969-1971 the 14in. (35.6cm) doll was also available as a child carrying a kitten. Legend was that they would sit together on the window seat, Jenny singing, the cat listening.

"Melinda" wears a gown of pink organdy with ten tiers of gathered pink lace. A pink rosebud adorns her pink ribbon sash. Her blonde hair has curls on her crown with tiny pink flowers. Her dress is tagged "Melinda." (Catalog #1173, 1969.) (*Maxine Salaman Collection.*)

"Melanie," catalog #1182, of 1970 is like "Melinda" except that her dress is yellow with several fewer rows of lace.

"Southern Belle" for 1971-1973 has a white organdy dress with four rows of lace on the skirt to give the appearance of tiers and lace-trimmed puff sleeves and neckline. Her straw hat has net and flower trim. She is wearing a heart necklace. Her dress is styled like that of the current 8in. (20.3cm) "Scarlett" and 14in. (35.6cm) "Gone With the Wind." She has brown hair and eyes. Her clothing is labeled "Southern Belle." (*Virginia Ann Heyerdahl Collection.*)

The "Southern Belle" of 1969 has the same dress with a *pink* sash and organdy hat with lace, flowers and pink ribbon. The 1970 version wears a *red* sash and red flowers on her organdy hat.

Left: "Godey" lady is very elegantly garbed in a natural straw hat, turned up on one side with flower trim topping her auburn hair. Her gown is pink taffeta covered with pink lace with two wide lace ruffles, one rising somewhat is the back. Her sash is pink satin, and she has pink lace trim at her neckline and sleeves. Her clothes are labeled "Godey." (Catalog #1183, 1970.) (*Maxine Salaman Collection.*)

Left: "Renoir" is wearing one of the loveliest creations in this whole Portrette series: an aqua satin gown with a print of tiny circles, which is different from the catalog which shows a stripe. The flounce at the front hem meets at the back waist. Her bodice is sleeveless with ecru lace to the neckline and armhole. Her matching velvet jacket has a link closing at the front and long sleeves edged with ecru lace. The matching velvet close-fitting hat has tulle and flower trim. This doll also came with a wider hat topped by a pouf of net. Her clothing is labeled "Madame Alexander." (Catalog #1180, 1970.) (*Maxine Salaman Collection.*)

Right: "Sleeping Beauty" was a special edition doll available only at Disneyland. She was like the "Cissette" doll but had flat feet, and the later dolls also had straight legs. She was available during the 1960s. "Sleeping Beauty" wears an aqua taffeta gown with a full skirt. Her bodice comes to a point in the center front and has a gold net covering. She wears a gold veil on her head, which is a replacement on the doll pictured. She is labeled on her clothing: "Walt Disney's Sleeping Beauty." (*Edna Black Collection.*)

V. Vinyl Head Dolls

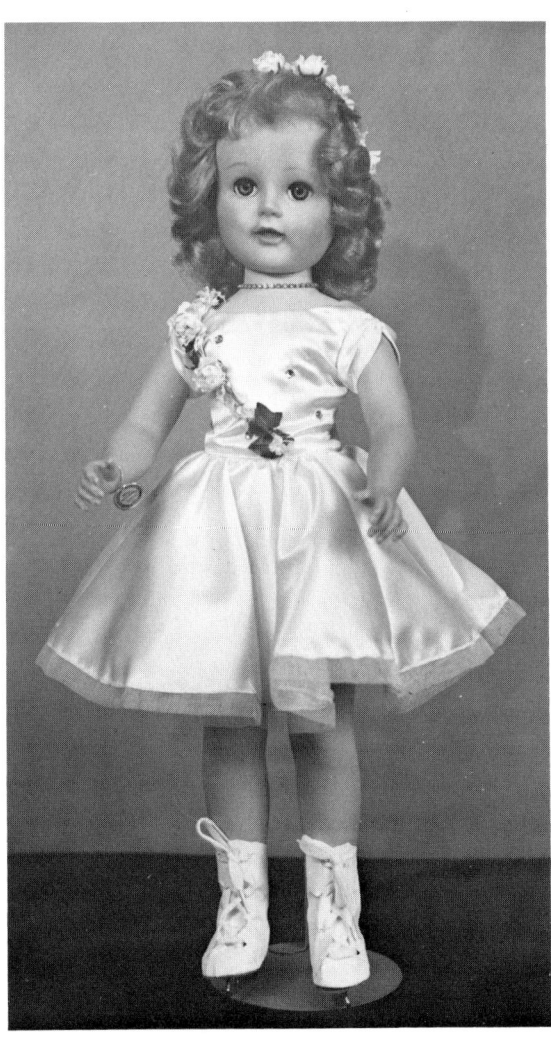

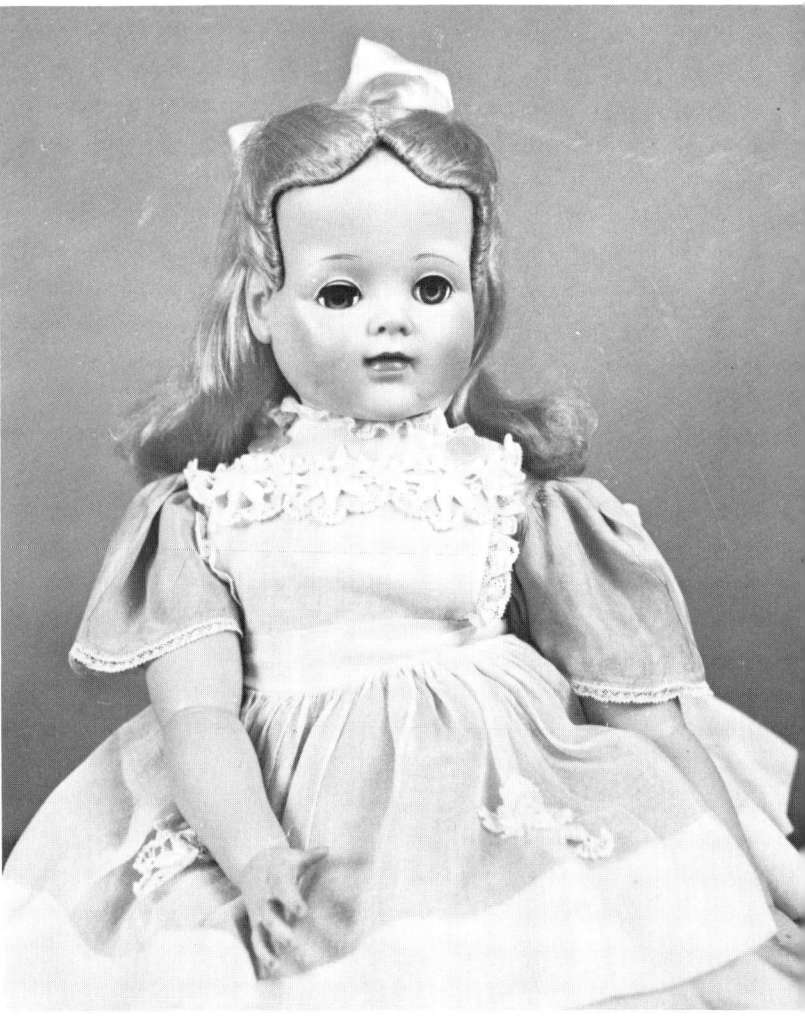

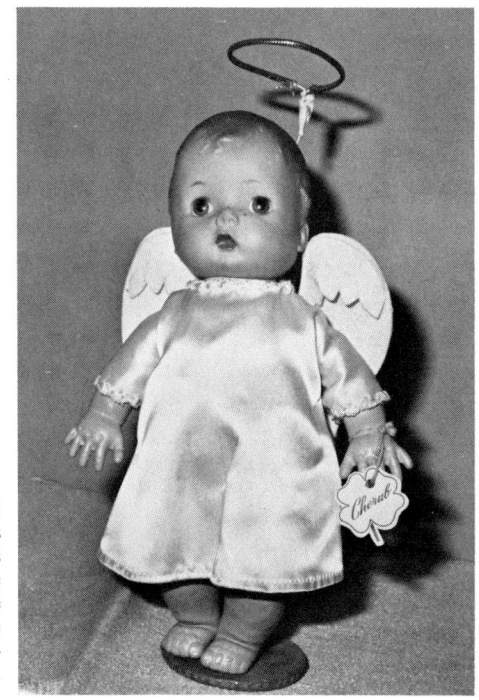

Above: "Sonja Henie" with the vinyl head was made in 1951 only. She was offered in 15in. (38.1cm), 18in. (45.7cm) and 23in. (58.4cm) sizes. With a new very appealing face, she was issued for the opening of the Sonja Henie Ice Revue. She has an open smiling mouth with no teeth and cute dimples. "Sonja Henie" is wearing a white satin dress with a rhinestone-studded bodice and a garland of flowers sweeping across her bodice. Her blonde curly hair has a band of flowers for ornamentation. Her head is marked "ALEXANDER" and her clothes are labeled "Madame Alexander." Her body is of hard plastic. The composition version of "Sonja Henie" is shown on page 38. (*Maxine Salaman Collection.*)

Above right: The 29in. (73.7cm) "Barbara Jane" doll introduced in the August 1950 *Playthings* ad was used to create this most lovely "Alice in Wonderland." Her vinyl head has soft and life-like features with blue lashed sleep eyes and very intricately molded ears. Her blonde hair is in the typical "Alice" style pulled up the sides and long in the back. Her body is cloth with vinyl arms and legs. Her blue taffeta dress tagged "Alice in Wonderland" is topped by a white organdy apron. She is marked on the head "ALEXANDER." (*Edna Black Collection.*)

"Cherub" is identified by his paper cloverleaf tag. He is 9in. (22.9cm) tall with a stuffed magic-skin-type body all of one piece. His vinyl head has molded and painted brown hair. His painted blue eyes are convex; he has some tiny freckles across his nose. Contributing to his cherubic appearance are his white satin gown edged with braid, his gold halo and his white wings, which make him a true "Cherub." The clothing label says "Madame Alexander." "Cherub" was purchased at John Wanamaker. He was advertised in the July 1950 *Playthings* as "The Littlest Cherub". (*Vivian C. Flagg Collection.*)

Madame Alexander began using soft plastic around 1950. It was used primarily for the baby dolls and for only a few of the child dolls. She continued using mainly hard plastic for the heads of the child dolls until the mid-1960s when she switched to vinyl heads but still retained the hard plastic bodies, except for the arms. She often used vinyl arms from the mid-1950s on.

In organizing dolls for this book, a doll is classifed as vinyl if the *head* is made of vinyl, regardless of the body material.

Left: "Madelaine" was introduced in the 1952 catalog, and was also made in 1953 and 1961. She was marked "ALEXANDER" on her vinyl head and came in one size, 18in. (45.7cm) only. She had a ball-jointed hard plastic body, just like the old German ones, completely jointed at the wrists, elbows, shoulders, knees and hips. There was a large selection of lovely clothes which could be purchased to fit her, and her hair could be washed, combed and curled. Here "Madelaine" is wearing an organdy dress with lots of lovely embroidery around the skirt, and a straw hat edged with lace. Her clothing is labeled "Madame Alexander." (*Maxine Salaman Collection.*)

"Flora McFlimsey" in this version with the vinyl head was made in 1953 only, catalog #1502. She was made only in the 15in. (38.1cm) size. Her body is hard plastic. Her eyes are sparkling blue with lashes and do not sleep. The 1953 catalog calls her "Miss Flora McFlimsey" and says she is "right out of the pages of Mariana's entrancing book about a little Victorian doll. Actually between 1949 and 1954, Mariana, who was really Marian Curtis Foster, wrote five books about Miss Flora McFlimsey. The catalog shows her in a white eyelet dress, but the "Flora McFlimsey" pictured here is wearing a yellow cotton dress with pink rosebuds which is also original. Her straw hat perches on top of her blonde and very curly hair. Her high-buttoned shoes and stockings are both black. (*Maxine Salaman Collection.*)

"Kelly" was a new face and personality introduced into the Alexander family in 1958. She came in 16in. (40.6cm) and 22in. (55.9cm) sizes. In 1959 she was also made in a 12in. (30.5cm) size with the "Lissy" face, which is shown on page 74. "Kelly" was manufactured with a vinyl head and arms, hard plastic torso and legs and a jointed waist. In this photo "Kelly," catalog #1900, is wearing a checked cotton dress with lace trim and tiny buttons, pocket decoration and puff sleeves. Her dress is labeled "Kelly." (*Edna Black Collection.*)

This "Pollyana," catalog #1530, is wearing a rose polished cotton dress with black braid trim and white collar and cuffs. Her straw hat with flower trim sits atop her blonde braided hair. Button shoes and long stockings complete her outfit. *(Maxine Salaman Collection.)*

The "Kelly" face was also used for "Pollyana" of 1960 and 1961. She also came in 16in. (40.6cm) and 22in.(55.9cm) sizes. "Pollyana," a mischievous yet immensely appealing child of turn of the century, is from the 1960 release of the *Pollyana* movie.

Dolls with the "Kelly" face are marked on the head:

MME © ALEXANDER
1958

This face was also used for "Marybel, the Doll Who Gets Well," and "Edith, the Lonely Doll."

A new face was created for "Maggie Mixup" of 1960. Her head is vinyl with straight red hair with bangs, green eyes and freckles, all of which give her an impish look. Her body is the same as that of "Elise" with hard plastic torso and legs, jointed even at the ankles, and vinyl arms jointed at the elbows.

Another cute face mold is that of "Miss Melinda" of 1962 and 1963. Her smiling open-closed mouth has two painted upper teeth. She came in 16in. (40.6cm) and 22in. (55.9cm) sizes with swivel waists, as well as a 14in. (35.6cm) size which did not swivel. Her head and arms are soft; the torso and legs are hard. "Melinda" was a part of Madame Alexander's fantasy world of pretend in that she was a doll who wrote letters. On the bottom of her wrist tag was a card that the child could tear off and send in to the company. Then the child would receive a letter from the doll on certain holidays. "Melinda" says: "I make believe that I write letters and when you receive them you can pretend that I really do."

This 16in. (40.6cm) "Miss Melinda" (called only "Melinda" in the catalog, #1512) is wearing a red velveteen bodice on a white organdy lace-edged skirt. Her fancy hat has flower and lace trim. Her clothes are tagged "Madame Alexander." Her head is marked:

ALEXANDER
19 © 62

(Maxine Salaman Collection.)

This "Maggie Mixup," catalog #1812, is wearing a turquoise and white checked skirt and white cotton blouse with puffed sleeves and lace trim. Her long black stockings and black slippers give her an old-fashioned look, as does her natural straw roller brim hat with turquoise ribbon trim. She is wearing a golden heart necklace which does not show in the picture. She also came in an 8in. (20.3cm) size, which is described on page 72. *(Maxine Salaman Collection.)*

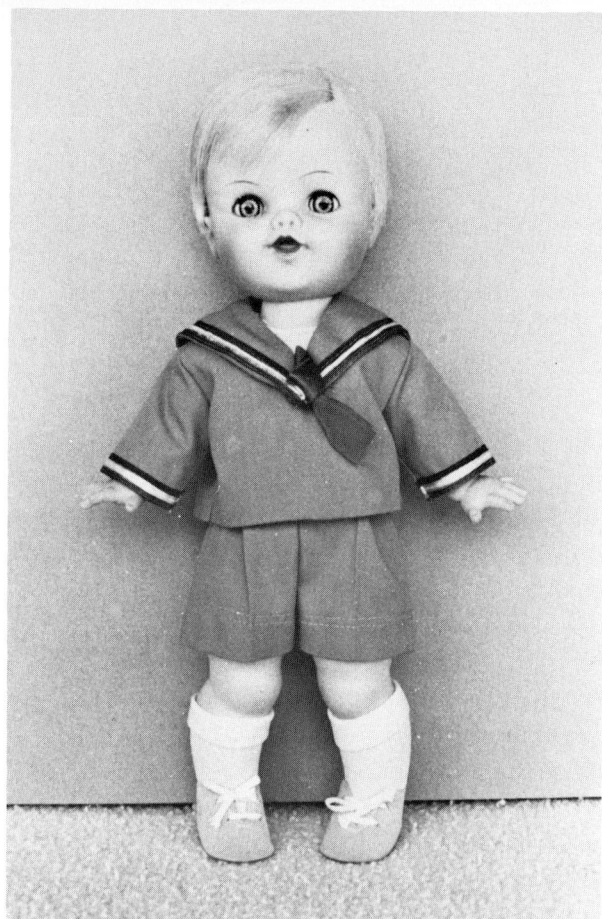

"Mary Ann," an adorable 14in. (35.6cm) sub-teen young lady, was a new doll and face in 1965. She has a vinyl head and a hard plastic body. As "Mary Ann" she was released for one year only, but the basic doll has been used extensively ever since then for a wide variety of dolls.

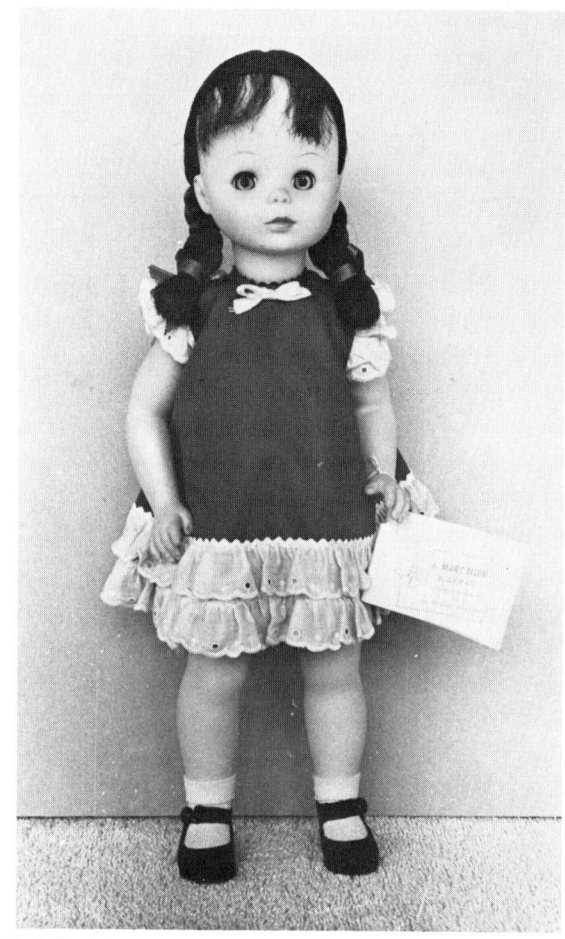

The "Smarty" doll was used for this 12in. (30.5cm) "Kurt" from the *Sound of Music*. He was made for only a very short time in the large *Sound of Music* set which had all of the children dressed in these blue sailor outfits. A photo from "Brigitta's" wrist booklet on page 76 shows the complete set. He is marked on the head: ALEXANDER
19 © 62
(*Rhoda Shoemaker Collection; photo courtesy of Rhoda Shoemaker.*)

This doll which uses the "Mary Ann" face is called "Mary Ellen Playmate." She was a special doll created by Madame Alexander as an exclusive for a store, such as Wanamaker or Marshall Field. She is not listed in any of the Alexander catalogs. "Mary Ellen" is wearing a dark wig with bangs and braids. Her red cotton dress is trimmed with white eyelet. Her snap shoes are also red. She is marked, as are all dolls with this face (regardless of the year in which they were put out):

ALEXANDER
19 © 65

(*Rhoda Shoemaker Collection; photo courtesy of Rhoda Shoemaker.*)

Another "Mary Ellen Playmate," is this 17in. (43.2cm) doll with the "Polly" face. She has a tag which reads "A Mary Ellen Playmate Created Exclusively for Us by Madame Alexander." She was bought at Wanamaker. "Mary Ellen" is wearing a blue polka dot dress with trim of blue and white stripes and her polka dot shoes match her dress. Her clothing is labeled "Madame Alexander." She is marked on the back of her head: © ALEXANDER DOLL CO. INC.
1965
She does not appear in any of the Alexander catalogs. (*Vivian C. Flagg Collection.*)

Considered by collectors as the most lovely and desirable of the modern Alexander doll creations is this "Coco" made only in 1966. The beautiful "Coco" was named for the famous Paris designer, Coco Chanel, originator of many innovative firsts in fashion and known for her suits and pants outfits. In the late 1960s work was beginning on a sumptuous Broadway musical based on her life, but when it opened, it did not become a hit. "Coco's" body is unusual: she has a hard plastic torso with jointed waist, hard plastic legs with the right one bent slightly at the knee and vinyl arms. This face was also used for the six portrait dolls of 1966: "Madame," "Godey," "Melanie," "Scarlett," "Lissy" and "Renoir."

"Coco" here, catalog #2030, is wearing a pink brocade sheath gown trimmed with matching pink maribou at sleeves and hem. This is an exact copy of the original. Her blonde hair is elegantly styled. (*Maxine Salaman Collection.*)

This 21in. (53.3cm) Ice Capades doll used the "Jacqueline" face designed in 1962 for the large Jacqueline Kennedy doll and since used extensively for the portrait dolls. Each year, the costume department of the Ice Capades dresses dolls to model the costume for each production number, so that the producers can visualize what each will look like. After the costumes are approved, the dolls are used in other technical planning for the show, such as set design and lighting. They are also used in advance publicity for the show. This doll's costume is bright turquoise with bead trim. Her skates are pasted on paper with turquoise trim. These models are not confined to Alexander dolls; dolls from many other companies are also used. (*Maxine Salaman Collection.*)

VI. Scarlett O'Hara, a Historical Perspective

On April 29, 1937 Madame Alexander was granted trademark #392,003 for "Scarlet [sic] O'Hara" dolls. As she was reading the novel, *Gone With the Wind*, she was impressed to design the "Scarlett O'Hara" doll, and received a contract with MGM to produce the dolls even before the film version of the runaway best seller was begun. "Scarlett" was to become another of Madame's most lasting and popular series beginning in the late 1930s and running almost continuously to the present, even spilling over into her "Melanie" dolls and her line of "Southern Belles." Also in 1937, she made "Carreen" and "Suellen," Scarlett's two sisters in 14in. (35.6cm) composition, and in 1957 she made "Aunt Pitty-Pat" in 8in. (20.3cm) hard plastic. The "Scarlett O'Hara" dolls are tops on many collectors' lists.

Although 100,000 copies were in print and distribution had begun in May, June 30, 1936 was the official publication day for *Gone with the Wind*. Booksellers were unable to keep their shelves stocked, most selling their books within a day or two of receipt. No advertising is better than word of mouth and people were scrambling over each other to pick up copies as soon as they appeared on the shelves. By the beginning of September, 370,000 copies were in print, and *Gone with the Wind* had broken all records as America's fastest selling book—probably the world's also. Within six months, 975,000 copies were in circulation.

Macmillan, the publishers, had advertised in the trade magazines, and at the official publication date had extensive ads in newspapers and magazines. This book, by Margaret Mitchell, a tiny lady from Atlanta, Georgia, had taken the nation by storm— quite a feat for a first novel, and incidently her last since she never wrote any others. In 1937 the book was awarded the Pulitzer Prize as the most distinguished novel of 1936.

The whole story of the publication of *Gone with the Wind* is fascinating. It was in 1926 while recuperating from an ankle injury that Miss Mitchell actually started writing her novel. In fact, she wrote the last chapter first so she knew in what direction her characters were headed from the very first. She kept her work a secret, but friends gradually realized she was working on some gigantic project. But since she had been a working professional journalist, no one was overly surprised to find she was writing a novel. As Miss Mitchell had always been fascinated by stories of the Civil War, the topic was a natural one for her. A friend of Miss Mitchell's worked for Macmillan and did indeed inform one of Macmillan's editors about Miss Mitchell's manuscript, although she had never been allowed to read it. Actually it was a taunt by another friend in 1935 which angered Miss Mitchell into showing the manuscript which she had kept by chapters in manila envelopes stored in various places throughout her apartment. And at the time she did show the manuscript to a Macmillan editor, she had not even written a beginning chapter. The next day she changed her mind and asked to have it returned, but the Macmillan editor was very much interested in possible publication after having read just parts of the manuscript.

Originally Miss Mitchell had called her heroine *Pansy*, but regarded this as a rather weak name for such a strong character. So delving back into the Irish history which she mentions in her book, she hit upon the name Scarlett, the name of a family who had fought for Irish freedom.

On July 7, 1936, David Selznick's offer of $50,000 for the film rights was accepted. It had been brought to his attention first in May by a story editor at Selznick International, after watching early sales trends. Miss Mitchell emphasized that she personally wanted nothing at all to do with the production of the film. Drawing room discussions centered around who would be chosen to play the leading roles; bets were even made. Selznick wanted Clark Gable for the part of Rhett Butler, so he had to make a deal with MGM for a share of the profits in exchange for the services of Gable as Rhett Butler. A talent search for the female lead kept the whole country interested as the hunt went on for two years until December 1938 when British actress Vivien Leigh was finally chosen after having had the inside track since February. It is said that Selznick even staged a discovery scene to convince the public that his talent search was legitimate. She came as a guest of Laurence Olivier, whom she was supposed to be visiting in this country, to the filming of the scenes of the burning of the Atlanta depot. Ever since then the story has circulated about how beautiful she looked as the fire lit her face which made Selznick think she might be right for the part, although in reality he had already chosen her.

The role was a grueling one on Miss Leigh through five months of six-day weeks, some days putting in as much as 18 hours. The complete film required about six months to complete. Her work was rewarded, however, as she won an Academy Award for her performance. The film debut was December 15, 1939, in Atlanta. The total cost including advertising had been $5,500,000.

The three costume variations from the film which appear most often on Madame Alexander's "Scarlett" dolls are the white dress with the many-flounced skirt which "Scarlett" wore in the opening scenes, the sprigged muslin with straw hat and parasol which she appeared in at the Wilkes barbecue at Twelve Oaks and the green velvet gown which she made from "Miss Ellen's portieres" so that she could go to Atlanta to borrow tax money from Rhett. Of course, these three were only a small number of the dozens of romantic costumes which Madame Alexander designed for "Scarlett." (Actually in the film Scarlett had 36 costume changes.)

Many of the Alexander designs for "Scarlett" are in green of different fabrics: cotton prints, satin, taffeta and velvet. This is appropriate since in the novel "Scarlett" did wear a lot of green. When asked about this, Miss Mitchell replied that she had not realized that Scarlett wore so much green, but was not surprised as green was her own favorite color.

The face chosen for the "Scarlett" doll was apparently new in 1937, and used at the same time for "Wendy Ann," "Carmen" and "Madelaine," and later for many, many others. It is a sweet heart-shaped face modeled after and named for Madame Alexander's granddaughter, Wendy Ann. The doll was all in composition usually with black hair and green eyes but there are some variations; she was made in a variety of sizes from 10in. (25.4cm) or 11in. (27.9cm) to 21in. (53.3cm). Dolls were made until 1942 as "Scarlett O'Hara"; from 1942-1945 a similar doll was called "Southern Girl."

1937 has been used for the beginning of the "Scarlett O'Hara" dolls because that was the date of the Alexander trademark, but the doll was not advertised in *Playthings* until the January to March issues of 1940, which would be when the film was still a new release. An April feature showed an F.A.O. Schwarz window full of "Scarlett" dolls.

Composition Scarletts

This beautiful 15in. (38.1cm) "Scarlett O'Hara" is dressed in a yellow print variation of the barbecue dress. This one has a scoop neckline, ruffles over the shoulders and around the cuffs and a flounce around the hem. She also is wearing her straw picture hat and pantaloons. (*Rosemary Dent Collection.*)

This dainty 11in. (27.9cm) "Scarlett O'Hara" wears a frock of yellow and green cotton print, a variation of the dress she wore to the barbecue. It has short puff sleeves, and a white organdy ruffle at the neckline. Her petticoat has a hoop to make her skirt stand out. She is wearing pantaloons and green shoes. Her natural straw picture hat has slid down behind her shoulders, and she has the typical black hair and green eyes. Her dress is tagged "Scarlett O'Hara." Her head is marked "ALEXANDER," but sometimes these dolls are not marked at all. (*Maxine Salaman Collection.*)

Here is an 18in. (45.7cm) "Scarlett O'Hara" in a traditional-style gown of gold taffeta with a dark velvet bodice, streamers and a band above the hem. The sleeves are gathered up to three-quarter length and are lace-edged, as is neckline. Her poke bonnet matches her dress. Again she is wearing a hoop skirt. (*Helen Teske Collection.*)

Another composition doll, this 14in. (35.6cm) "Scarlett O'Hara" is wearing a frock of pale pink silk organza held out by a hoop skirt and trimmed by a ribbon sash and lace edging at the cuffs and neckline. Her bonnet matches her dress. (*Rhoda Shoemaker Collection; photo courtesy of Rhoda Shoemaker.*)

The next version of "Scarlett O'Hara" was issued in the suntanned hard plastic probably in 1949 or 1950, using the "Margaret" face.

One of the loveliest of all the "Scarletts," this 14in. (35.6cm) doll is wearing a light green organdy dress covered by a green taffeta coat with a very full gathered waist. The long sleeves are gathered all the way from the shoulders to the wrists. Delicate lace trims the large collar and cuffs. Her matching fabric bonnet has a row of lace framing her face and a large bouquet of pink-toned flowers for decoration. Her hair is jet black, and her eyes are gray. Her dress is tagged "Madame Alexander." (*Maxine Salaman Collection.*)

From 1955 to 1957 the small 7-1/2in. (19.1 cm) or 8in. (20.3cm) "Wendy" was available with a "Scarlett O'Hara" outfit. These were darling dolls with lovely outfits.

In 1955 "Scarlett," catalog #485, wore a flower sprigged muslin, trimmed with braid and tiny bows. Her frock had puff sleeves of tulle and a large flower-trimmed picture hat of straw.

In 1956, catalog #631, she wore a frock of muslin with a rosebud print and a scoop neckline with lace edging. She carried a parasol and wore her large picture hat.

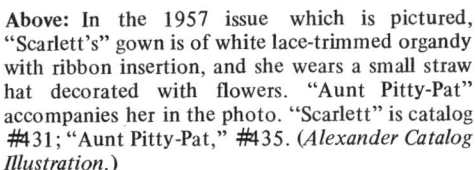

Above: In the 1957 issue which is pictured, "Scarlett's" gown is of white lace-trimmed organdy with ribbon insertion, and she wears a small straw hat decorated with flowers. "Aunt Pitty-Pat" accompanies her in the photo. "Scarlett" is catalog #431; "Aunt Pitty-Pat," #435. (*Alexander Catalog Illustration.*)

Upper right: Madame Alexander designed a beautiful blue taffeta dress for the 21in. (53.3cm) "Scarlett" of 1961 with the "Cissy" face, catalog #2240. Her gown has a very full skirt which is trimmed around the hem with looped black braid. Her jacket with long sleeves and hip length pointed panels in front and in back, is also trimmed with black braid. Her bonnet is of matching blue taffeta with flower trim and black ties. "Scarlett" is wearing black lace mitts and is carrying a black reticule. (*Alexander Catalog Illustration.*)

Below right: One 1963 "Scarlett O'Hara," catalog #1256, used the "Lissy" face. For this 12in. (30.5cm) version Madame Alexander designed a green taffeta frock with very full skirt and bodice of white organdy trimmed with lace and tiny buttons. Her green taffeta jacket has white lace peeking out from her sleeves and is outlined with braid trim. Her matching bonnet with the same trim also has flowers and a braid bow tying under her chin. Unlike many "Scarletts," this one has blue eyes. Her dress is tagged "Madame Alexander." (*Maxine Salaman Collection.*)

Another 1963 "Scarlett" is this 18in. (45.7cm) beauty using the "Elise" face, catalog #1760. Her gown is very different from that of any other "Scarlett." It is of pale blue organdy. Down the front are three panels of vertical tucks and rows of lace trim. Her sleeves, which are very full at the bottoms, are also trimmed with tucks and lace. Her blue satin sash cascades down her back. Rosebuds trim her sash and the front of her dress. Her natural straw picture hat is trimmed with flowers and ties under her chin. Truly a lovely doll! (*Alexander Catalog Illustration.*)

In 1965, Madame Alexander began the 21in. (53.3cm) Portrait Series with the use of the "Jacqueline" face. Although the dolls offered change almost yearly, this series is still in production today. Of course, a "Scarlett" was included in this first set, catalog #2152. She is dressed in green satin with a billowing full skirt. The dress has a vee neck with lace and black ribbon insertion trim; her below-the-elbow sleeves are also trimmed with lace and black ribbon insertion. Her natural straw picture hat has flower trim. Her eyes are blue. (*Alexander Catalog Illustration.*)

Again in 1965, Madame Alexander began issuing a small 8in. (20.3cm) "Scarlett," catalog #785. For this first year only "Scarlett" wore a white taffeta dress with a full skirt; a ruffle circled the hem with green rickrack trim and a tiny rose at the side. Her elbow-length sleeves are also trimmed with green rickrack and lace and her ribbon sash is green. She is wearing her usual natural straw flower-trimmed hat. Her eyes are green. Her dress is tagged "Scarlett O'Hara." (*Virginia Ann Heyerdahl Collection.*)

In 1966, the "Scarlett" doll was issued in the 21in. (53.3cm) size with the "Coco" face, catalog #2061. This is the only year the "Coco" face was used. This gorgeous "Scarlett" has a white tulle dress with a wide lace insertion around the bottom of the skirt. She has a red sash with red rose trim on it and on her skirt. Her white horsehair hat is trimmed with white flowers. The doll has brown eyes. (*Alexander Catalog Illustration.*)

From 1966 until 1972, the small 8in. (20.3 cm) "Scarlett," catalog #725, wore the same style dress in a variety of prints nearly always in green. The catalog does not show the changing print of the fabric, so these are nearly impossible to date specifically. The gown is made with a full skirt with a ruffle at the bottom and a row of rickrack at the top and bottom of the ruffle. Lace edges the scoop neck and puff sleeves. The accessories of the dress include a green satin sash and natural straw hat. All of these dolls have black hair and green eyes; they all have bending knees, but do not walk. The clothes are labeled "Scarlett O'Hara" or simply "Scarlett." (*Jackie Dent Collection.*)

Another print gown, this one with turquoise flowers and green leaves. (*Virginia Ann Heyerdahl Collection.*)

This print variation has green leaves and pink flowers. (*Virginia Ann Heyerdahl Collection.*)

This is the Portrette "Scarlett" using the 10in. (25.4cm) "Cissette" doll with the glamorized eyes, issued from 1968-1973. The costume for all six years was basically the same with some variation in the color and placement of the braid trim. Her frock is emerald green with a very full skirt trimmed with black braid. The separate jacket has lace around the cuffs of the long sleeves, and braid all around the jacket edges. Her matching bonnet with stiff brim and gathered crown has a flower corsage on one side. In 1970-1973, she wore a cameo necklace. Her dress is tagged "Scarlett." She has brown hair and green eyes. (*Virginia Ann Heyerdahl Collection.*)

Also in 1968, "Scarlett" was again offered as a 21in. (53.3cm) Portrait doll, catalog #2180. This time she is wearing a sleeveless muslin dress with yellow flower print. A flounce of white organdy with green ribbon insertion circles the bottom of the skirt. Around her vee neck is a wide ruffle edged with lace and ribbon insertion. Again she is wearing a natural straw hat with green ribbon ties, and is carrying her parasol. (*Alexander Catalog Illustration.*)

Still in 1968, two other versions of "Scarlett" were offered. Though this 14in. (35.6cm) version with the "Mary Ann" face is labeled "Gone With The Wind" she is definitely a "Scarlett," and she is still available. Her white organdy dress has a full skirt with five rows of lace to give the appearance of tiers. Lace trims her bodice and puff sleeves. Her sash is green velvet with a rhinestone ornament. Her hairbows which hold back her long wavy hair are also green. She is catalog #1490. (*Beth Foulke Collection.*)

A companion "Scarlett," also offered in 1968, catalog #1495, and using the 14in. (35.6cm) doll with the "Mary Ann" face, is this one wearing a sprigged muslin dress with a green velvet sash ending in long streamers at the back hem. Her natural straw hat is also trimmed with green velvet ribbons. She is a very difficult doll to find, being made for only one year. (*Alexander Catalog Illustration.*)

"Scarlett" again wears an emerald green gown with a very full skirt. Her matching jacket is long with points at the front and back. White braid trims jacket and skirt, and the sleeves are edged in white lace. Her poke bonnet brim decorated with a flower corsage and having a gathered crown ties under the chin. She is wearing a gold heart necklace. This is the 1969 version, catalog #2190. The 1967 version, catalog #2174, has black braid trim; 1970, catalog #2180, has white braid trim applied with rounded curves. (*Virginia Ann Heyerdahl Collection.*)

The 21in. (53.3cm) Portrait "Scarlett" was made from 1975 to 1977 in basically the same style as the 1969 one. Green braid trim is used around the edges of the jacket. Her bonnet is fuller at the crown and the brim is now fringed. Her hair is styled with long curls and her eyes are green. The catalog number for 1975 is #2292; for 1976 it is #2295; and for 1977 it is #2296. (*Virginia Ann Heyerdahl Collection.*)

Here is the current 8in. (20.3cm) "Scarlett" which has been in production since 1973, catalog #425. She is again wearing the white organdy dress with a full skirt and three rows of lace to give the appearance of tiers. Lace trims each side of her bodice and edges her puff sleeves. A green satin sash with tiny ornament circles her waist; her hair ribbons match. Her hair is dark, and her eyes are green. Her dress is tagged "Scarlett." (*Virginia Ann Heyerdahl Collection.*)

Regarded by many as the most beautiful of all the "Scarletts" ever created by Madame Alexander is this 21in. (53.3cm) Portrait for 1978 only, catalog #2210. Her gown is satin with pink printed roses and green leaves. Her parasol and satin sash are emerald green. Her natural straw hat is decorated with green satin ribbons and a corsage of roses. The neckline of her dress is wide and comes to a vee. It is banded with a matching satin ruffle with lace edging, and insertion containing green ribbon runs along the neckline and ruffle edge. "Scarlett" is wearing an emerald pendant necklace and a sparkling ring. Her eyes are green, and her dark hair is styled in long curls. (*Beth Foulke Collection.*)

For 1979, Madame Alexander has announced a new Portrait "Scarlett" in the 21in. (53.3cm) size. She wears a green velvet gown with lace cap sleeves and braid trim. Her matching bustle-length jacket is trimmed with braid, and ecru lace edges the cuffs. She wears an emerald green stone on gold-colored chain around her neck and a diamond-like ring on her finger. Her hair is styled in elegant shoulder-length curls; her eyes are green. (*Alexander Catalog Illustration.*)

A Chronology Of Madame Alexander's Scarlett O'Hara

1937-1942....... Composition 10in. (25.4cm) or 11in. (27.9cm) to 21in. (53.3cm) using "Wendy Ann" face. Costumes in a variety of styles.

Ca.1949-1950......... Hard plastic 14in. (35.6cm), perhaps other sizes as well, using "Margaret" face.

1955......... Hard plastic 7-1/2in. (19.1cm), #485, print gown.

1956......... Hard plastic 8in. (20.3cm), #631, print gown.

1957......... Hard plastic 8in. (20.3cm), #431, white organdy.

1961......... Hard plastic 21in. (53.3cm) using "Cissy" face, #2240, blue taffeta.

1963......... Hard plastic 18in. (45.7cm) using "Elise" face, #1760, pale blue organdy.

1963......... Hard plastic 12in. (30.5cm) using "Lissy" face, #1256, green taffeta.

1965......... Vinyl 21in. (53.3cm) using "Jacqueline" face, #2152, green satin.

1965......... Hard plastic 8in. (20.3cm), #785, white taffeta.

1966......... Vinyl 21in. (53.3cm) using "Coco" face, #2061, white tulle and lace.

1966-1972........ Hard plastic 8in. (20.3cm), #725, various green sprigged calico gowns.

1967,1969,1970..... Vinyl 21in. (53.3cm) using "Jacqueline" face, #2174, #2190, #2180, green taffeta.

1968......... Vinyl 21in. (53.3cm) using "Jacqueline" face, #2180, print dress.

1968......... Vinyl 14in. (35.6cm) using "Mary Ann" face, #1495, print gown.

1968......... Vinyl 14in. (35.6cm) using "Mary Ann" face, #1490, later #1590, white organdy.*

1968-1973......... Hard plastic 12in. (30.5cm) using "Cissette" face, #1174, #1181, green taffeta.

1973......... Hard plastic 8in. (20.3cm) #425, white organdy.*

1975-1977......... Vinyl 21in. (53.3cm) using "Jacqueline" face, #2292, #2295, #2296, green taffeta.

1978......... Vinyl 21in. (53.3cm) using "Jacqueline" face, #2210, print satin.

1979......... Vinyl 21in. (53.3cm) using "Jacqueline" face, green velvet.

*Indicates still in production.

Index

A
Agatha, 82
Agnes, cloth, 10
Alexander-Kins, hard plastic, 69-74
Alice in Wonderland, 85
  cloth, 7
  composition, 33, 35, 53
  hard plastic, 41, 74
  vinyl and cloth, 56
American Girl, hard plastic, 73
Amish Boy, hard plastic, 73
Amish Girl, hard plastic, 73
Annabell, hard plastic, 42

B
Babbie, cloth, 10
Babs, hard plastic, 47
Baby McGuffey, 49
Barbara Jane, 85
Betty, composition, 35
Binnie (Walker), hard plastic, 59
Bride, hard plastic, 47
Bridesmaid, composition, 32
Brigitta, hard plastic, 76

C
Cherub, 84
Cinderella, hard plastic, 50, 52, 77
Cissette, 79, 81
Cissy, hard plastic, 60, 61, 62-65
Clarabell, cloth, 12
Coco, 89
Cynthia, hard plastic, 51

D
David Copperfield, cloth, 10
Dionne Quintuplets, composition, 17-22, 56
Dopey, 5

E
Edith, 87
Elise, hard plastic, 66

F
Fairy Princess, composition, 31, 32
Fairy Queen, composition, 34
  hard plastic, 46
Finnish, composition, 23
First Communion, hard plastic, 71
Flora McFlimsey, 86
  composition, 28

G
Gibson Girl, 81
Glamour Girls, hard plastic, 1, 57-58
Godey, 56, 82, 84
Godey Bride, 52
Godey Lady, hard plastic, 51, 54, 55
Gold Rush, 81
Gretel, composition, 34, 49

H
Hansel, composition, 49
  hard plastic, 34

I
Ice Capades, 89
International Series
  composition, 23
  hard plastic, 69

J
Jacqueline, 80
Jane Withers, composition, 36, 37, 53
Jeannie Walker, composition, 39
Jenny Lind, 83
Judy, composition, 33

K
Kate Greenaway, composition, 28, 29, 49
Kathy, hard plastic, 41
Katie, hard plastic, 75
Kelly, 86, 87
  hard plastic, 74, 75
Klondike, 81
Kurt, 88

L
Laurie, hard plastic, 53, 72, 77, 78
Lissy, hard plastic, 74
Little Colonel, composition, 24
Little Dorrit, cloth, 10
Little Em'ly, cloth, 10, 49
Little Genius, hard plastic, 67
Little Nell, cloth, 11
Little Shavers, cloth, 12
Little Women, cloth, 8, 9
  hard plastic, 44, 53, 72, 77-78
Littlest Cherub, 85

M
Madelaine, 86
  composition, 31
Madelaine du Bain, composition, 31
Maggie Mixup, hard plastic, 72, 87
Maggie (Walker), hard plastic, 40
Margaret O'Brien,
  composition, 33
  hard plastic, 45
Margaret Rose, hard plastic, 47
Margot, 79
Marionettes, 13-16
Mary Ann, 88
Marybel, 86
Mary Ellen, hard plastic, 60
Mary Ellen Playmate, 88
Mary Martin, hard plastic, 48
McGuffey Ana,
  composition, 23, 26, 27, 52, 53
  hard plastic, 46, 56, 76
Melinda, 82, 83, 87
Miss America, composition, 32, 49
Miss Flora McFlimsey, 86
Miss Melinda, 87

N
Nat, hard plastic, 42
Nina Ballerina, hard plastic, 3, 48
Nurse, composition, 25

O
Oliver Twist, cloth, 10

P
Pamela, hard plastic, 75
Peter Pan, hard plastic, 42
Pollyana, 87
Polly Pigtails, hard plastic, 41
Pip, cloth, 10
Piper Laurie, hard plastic, 50
Prince Charming, hard plastic, 50, 52
Princess Elizabeth, composition, 25

R
Red Riding Hood, cloth, 11
Renoir, 82, 84
Ringbearer, hard plastic, 67
Rosamund Bridesmaid, hard plastic, 1, 43

S
Sarg, Tony, 13
Scarlett O'Hara, 1, 90-102
Shari Lewis, hard plastic, 68
Sleeping Beauty, 84
  hard plastic, 68
Smarty, 88
Snow White, composition, 28
  hard plastic, 74
So-Lite, cloth, 11
Sonja Henie, 85
  composition, 38
Sound of Music, 76, 88

continued on page 104

Southern Belle, 81, 83
   hard plastic, 71, 76
Special Girl, composition, 40
Storyland, hard plastic, 69
Stuffy, hard plastic, 42
Sweet Violet, hard plastic, 59
Swiss, composition, 23

T

Tiny Tim, cloth, 10

Tommy, hard plastic, 75
Tommy Bangs, hard plastic, 42

V

Victoria, hard plastic, 70

W

Wendy Ann,
   composition, 30, 31, 52
   hard plastic, 69, 70, 71

Wendy-kin, hard plastic, 69
Winnie (Walker), hard plastic, 59
Winsome Binnie Walker, hard plastic, 59
Winsome Winnie Walker, hard plastic, 59

Y

Yardley Ads, 62-65

Bibliography

Flamini, Roland, *Scarlett, Rhett, and a Cast of Thousands,* Collier Books, Div. of Macmillan Publishing Co., Inc., New York, 1975.

Pratt, William, *Scarlett Fever*, Collier Books, Div. MacMillan Publishing Co., Inc., New York, 1977.

Other Books by Author

1st BLUE BOOK OF DOLLS & VALUES
2nd BLUE BOOK OF DOLLS & VALUES
3rd BLUE BOOK OF DOLLS & VALUES
Focusing On EFFANBEE COMPOSITION DOLLS
Focusing On HEUBACH CHARACTER DOLLS